Circular Economy and Ecosystem Restoration: A Sustainable Approach to Land Management, Climate Change Solutions, Water Security, Biodiversity Conservation, and Waste Reduction

Copyright

Circular Economy and Ecosystem Restoration: A Sustainable Approach to Land Management, Climate Change Solutions, Water Security, Biodiversity Conservation, and Waste Reduction

© 2025 Robert C. Brears

The author and publisher are of the same opinion regarding the views and content expressed in this work.

Disclaimer: The information in this book is provided for general knowledge and educational purposes only. While every effort has been made to ensure accuracy, the author and publisher make no representations or warranties with respect to the completeness or suitability of the content. The author and publisher accept no liability for any errors, omissions, or outcomes resulting from the application of information contained herein. Readers are advised to consult appropriate professionals or authorities before acting on any material presented.

ISBN (eBook): 978-1-991369-73-4

ISBN (Paperback): 978-1-991369-74-1

Published by Global Climate Solutions

First Edition, 2025

Cover design and interior layout by Global Climate Solutions

Table of Contents

Introduction

Ecosystems provide essential services, including carbon
sequestration, water purification, biodiversity support, and soil
regeneration. However, industrialization, urban expansion,
deforestation, and unsustainable resource extraction have led to
severe environmental degradation, weakening ecosystems and
reducing their ability to sustain life. Conventional economic systems
operate on a linear model—extract, produce, consume, and
discard—which accelerates resource depletion and waste
accumulation.

The circular economy presents a transformative alternative by
closing resource loops, reducing waste, and promoting regenerative
practices. Rather than a one-way flow of materials, the circular
economy emphasizes reuse, recycling, repair, and biological
regeneration to extend the lifespan of resources while minimizing
environmental harm.

Integrating circular economy principles into ecosystem restoration
enhances natural resilience by aligning human activities with
nature's regenerative cycles. Restoration efforts based on circularity
focus on reducing pollution, conserving natural resources, reusing
materials, and regenerating degraded environments. These
approaches go beyond traditional conservation by actively repairing
ecological damage while ensuring long-term sustainability.

This book explores how circular economy strategies can be applied
to restore ecosystems, providing solutions for land degradation,
water scarcity, biodiversity loss, and climate resilience. By
leveraging circular principles, societies can restore ecosystems while
maintaining economic prosperity, ensuring that natural and human
systems coexist harmoniously.

Importance of Integrating Circularity into Restoration Efforts

Ecosystem restoration has traditionally focused on mitigating damage rather than preventing future degradation. Many restoration projects rely on one-time interventions, such as replanting forests, rehabilitating rivers, or cleaning up polluted areas. While these efforts provide short-term relief, they often fail to address the root causes of degradation, such as unsustainable resource consumption, industrial waste, and inefficient land use.

Integrating circular economy principles into restoration efforts ensures that ecosystems are not only repaired but also maintained in a self-sustaining manner. Circular restoration shifts from a reactive approach to a proactive and regenerative model, focusing on:

- Waste reduction and resource efficiency, ensuring that restoration efforts minimize environmental footprints.
- Nature-based solutions, such as regenerative agriculture, bio-based materials, and wetland restoration, to enhance ecosystem resilience.
- Closed-loop systems, where materials, water, and energy are continuously reused, reducing extraction pressures on natural ecosystems.
- Long-term economic and social benefits, providing financial incentives for businesses and communities to support sustainable restoration.

By embedding circularity into restoration initiatives, societies can prevent recurring environmental damage, enhance biodiversity, and improve climate resilience. The following chapters will explore practical applications of circular economy strategies in ecosystem restoration, offering innovative and scalable solutions for a sustainable future.

Chapter 1: Understanding Circular Economy in Ecosystem Restoration

Ecosystems are the foundation of life, providing essential services such as water purification, carbon storage, biodiversity support, and soil fertility. However, decades of unsustainable practices—driven by linear economic models that prioritize extraction, consumption, and disposal—have led to environmental degradation, habitat loss, and resource depletion. Conventional restoration efforts, while necessary, often focus on damage control rather than long-term resilience.

The circular economy offers a transformative approach by integrating waste reduction, resource efficiency, and regenerative practices into environmental restoration. Unlike the traditional "take-make-dispose" model, circular strategies emphasize closed-loop systems where materials, nutrients, and resources are continuously reused or regenerated. This approach not only restores degraded ecosystems but also prevents future environmental damage by embedding sustainability into economic and industrial processes.

This chapter explores the key principles of the circular economy, examining how they apply to ecosystem restoration. It also discusses the role of circularity in mitigating ecological damage and identifies the challenges and opportunities associated with implementing circular restoration initiatives. By understanding the foundations of circular thinking, we can develop scalable, long-term solutions that restore ecosystems while supporting economic sustainability.

Key Principles of the Circular Economy

The circular economy is an alternative to the traditional linear economic model, which follows a take-make-dispose approach, leading to resource depletion, excessive waste, and environmental degradation. In contrast, a circular economy is designed to mimic natural ecosystems, where materials and energy continuously cycle, ensuring long-term sustainability.

By focusing on waste prevention, material recovery, and regenerative systems, circular economy principles help reduce pressure on natural resources while enhancing ecosystem resilience. This section explores the core principles that guide circular economic strategies and their role in ecosystem restoration.

Designing Out Waste and Pollution

A foundational principle of the circular economy is eliminating waste at the source rather than managing it after it has been created. In linear systems, waste is often seen as an unavoidable byproduct, but in a circular system, it is treated as a design flaw that must be corrected.

Key Strategies for Waste Prevention:

- **Eco-design and material efficiency**: Products and infrastructure are designed to be long-lasting, reusable, and recyclable, reducing waste accumulation.
- **Industrial symbiosis**: Waste from one process is used as a resource in another, ensuring materials remain in productive use.
- **Biodegradable and non-toxic materials**: Replacing hazardous chemicals and single-use plastics with compostable alternatives minimizes long-term pollution.

By preventing waste and pollution at the design stage, ecosystems are less burdened by contamination, improving their ability to regenerate naturally.

Keeping Products and Materials in Use

Circularity prioritizes extending the lifecycle of products, materials, and resources, reducing the need for new extraction. This principle shifts the focus from constant consumption to reuse, repair, refurbishment, and recycling.

Circular Strategies for Keeping Resources in Use:

- **Reuse and remanufacturing**: Instead of discarding products, they are repaired, upgraded, or repurposed to extend their lifespan.
- **Material recovery and recycling**: Valuable materials, such as metals, plastics, and biomass, are collected and reintegrated into production cycles.
- **Sharing and leasing models**: Shifting from product ownership to service-based access (e.g., shared transportation, equipment leasing) reduces material demand.

By keeping materials in circulation for as long as possible, ecosystems face less resource extraction pressure, allowing degraded environments to recover.

Regenerating Natural Systems

Unlike traditional economic models that deplete resources, a circular economy actively restores and enhances ecosystems. This principle focuses on building natural resilience by ensuring that land, water, and biodiversity are continuously regenerated.

Approaches to Regenerative Practices:

- **Regenerative agriculture**: Using techniques such as crop rotation, cover cropping, and reduced tillage to restore soil health.
- **Sustainable forestry**: Implementing selective logging and reforestation to maintain carbon sequestration and biodiversity.

- **Water cycle restoration**: Enhancing wetland filtration, groundwater recharge, and nature-based flood control solutions to ensure water availability.

By integrating regenerative strategies, circular systems work with nature rather than against it, enabling long-term ecological recovery.

Transitioning to Renewable Resources and Energy

Circular systems prioritize the use of renewable resources over finite, non-renewable materials. Shifting from fossil fuels and non-renewable raw materials to bio-based, renewable, and low-carbon alternatives reduces environmental impact.

Key Renewable Resource Strategies:

- Replacing fossil-based materials with bio-based plastics, natural fibers, and biodegradable packaging.
- Prioritizing renewable energy sources, such as solar, wind, and hydropower, to power industrial processes and communities.
- Developing sustainable bioeconomy solutions, where biological materials (e.g., algae, agricultural waste) are used for fuel, food, and bioplastics.

By reducing dependency on finite resources, circular models lower carbon emissions, decrease pollution, and preserve ecosystems.

How Circular Approaches Apply to Environmental Restoration

Environmental restoration seeks to rehabilitate degraded ecosystems, ensuring they regain their ability to support biodiversity, regulate climate, and provide essential ecosystem services such as clean air, water filtration, and soil fertility. However, many restoration efforts are temporary fixes that do not address the underlying causes of degradation, such as unsustainable resource extraction, pollution, and waste accumulation.

The circular economy offers a transformative solution by integrating waste reduction, resource efficiency, and regenerative practices into environmental restoration. Unlike traditional approaches that focus solely on damage control, circular strategies create self-sustaining ecosystems that recover naturally over time while minimizing further environmental impact.

This section explores how circular economy principles can be applied to ecosystem restoration, focusing on material reuse, pollution reduction, nature-based solutions, and resource-efficient restoration projects.

Restoring Ecosystems Through Resource Efficiency

Circular economy principles prioritize using fewer resources while maximizing their longevity and efficiency. In environmental restoration, this means reducing the demand for new raw materials while improving existing resource management.

Circular Strategies for Resource-Efficient Restoration:

- **Reusing natural materials**: Instead of extracting virgin materials, restoration efforts can use reclaimed wood, recycled aggregates, and biodegradable plant-based products for soil stabilization and reforestation.
- **Minimizing waste in restoration projects**: Construction and landscape restoration efforts should use low-waste techniques to prevent landfill accumulation.
- **Applying closed-loop systems**: Water used in ecological restoration can be collected, treated, and reused rather than extracted from limited freshwater sources.

By conserving materials and energy, restoration efforts become more cost-effective and environmentally responsible.

Pollution Reduction and Circular Waste Management

Pollution is one of the primary causes of ecosystem degradation, contaminating water bodies, soils, and air. A circular approach to pollution management ensures that waste is minimized, repurposed, or treated before it harms the environment.

Applying Circular Solutions to Pollution Reduction:

- **Recovering and repurposing waste**: Waste from industrial and agricultural activities can be converted into fertilizers, biochar, or alternative construction materials for restoration projects.
- **Utilizing bioremediation techniques**: Microorganisms, plants, and fungi can be used to break down pollutants and regenerate soil health.
- **Preventing future contamination**: Circular waste management ensures that harmful materials do not enter ecosystems, promoting long-term ecological stability.

By shifting from a pollution-control mindset to a pollution-prevention strategy, circular approaches enhance ecosystem resilience.

Integrating Nature-Based Solutions into Restoration

Traditional restoration projects often rely on hard infrastructure, such as concrete barriers for flood control or artificial soil treatments. In contrast, circular restoration mimics and enhances natural processes, ensuring that ecosystems restore themselves over time.

Nature-Based Circular Approaches to Restoration:

- **Wetland restoration for water purification**: Natural wetlands filter pollutants, store excess rainwater, and support biodiversity more effectively than artificial drainage systems.
- **Reforestation and agroforestry**: Planting diverse species in degraded lands improves soil fertility, retains water, and sequesters carbon, offering long-term environmental benefits.
- **Green infrastructure**: Using living walls, urban forests, and permeable pavements helps cities adapt to climate change while restoring local ecosystems.

By utilizing nature-based strategies, circular restoration ensures long-term environmental and social benefits.

Circular Design in Restoration Planning and Implementation

Circular economy principles also influence how restoration projects are designed, planned, and executed. Restoration efforts must prioritize regenerative solutions that do not create new environmental burdens.

Key Circular Design Approaches for Restoration:

- **Adaptive reuse of degraded land**: Instead of leaving abandoned industrial sites contaminated, they can be repurposed into parks, wetlands, or renewable energy hubs.
- **Sustainable materials in restoration projects**: Using bio-based, non-toxic, and recyclable materials prevents long-term ecological damage.
- **Long-term monitoring and adaptive management**: Restoration efforts should be continuously evaluated to ensure they remain effective and do not require excessive resource inputs over time.

By embedding circular thinking into restoration planning, ecosystems can recover in a self-sustaining manner, reducing the need for constant human intervention.

The Role of Circularity in Mitigating Ecological Damage

Human activities have significantly altered natural ecosystems, leading to widespread habitat destruction, biodiversity loss, and climate change. The traditional linear economy—based on extracting, consuming, and discarding resources—has intensified these environmental challenges by increasing waste production, pollution, and resource depletion.

The circular economy offers a systemic solution to these issues by shifting economic activities toward waste prevention, material reuse, and regenerative resource management. Instead of treating environmental damage as an unavoidable consequence of development, circularity ensures that human activities actively contribute to ecological restoration and long-term sustainability.

This section explores how circular economy principles can mitigate ecological damage by reducing resource depletion, minimizing pollution, enhancing biodiversity, and improving climate resilience.

Reducing Resource Depletion and Land Degradation

Over-extraction of natural resources—such as deforestation, excessive mining, and unsustainable agriculture—has led to the degradation of land and water systems. Circular economy strategies reduce pressure on ecosystems by promoting efficient resource use and regenerative practices.

Circular Approaches to Reduce Resource Depletion:

- **Recycling and material recovery**: Closing resource loops by reprocessing materials such as metals, glass, and plastics reduces the need for virgin resource extraction.

- **Sustainable sourcing**: Using biodegradable, bio-based, and renewable materials minimizes long-term environmental impact.
- **Eco-friendly production models**: Businesses adopting zero-waste manufacturing and lean production techniques prevent excessive land and resource exploitation.

By minimizing reliance on new raw materials, circularity helps prevent soil degradation, deforestation, and biodiversity loss, allowing ecosystems to regenerate.

Minimizing Pollution and Waste Accumulation

Traditional waste management systems often rely on landfilling and incineration, which contribute to air, water, and soil pollution. The circular economy aims to eliminate waste at the source by designing systems where materials remain in continuous use.

Circular Strategies for Pollution Reduction:

- **Industrial symbiosis**: Waste from one industry serves as a raw material for another, reducing overall waste production.
- **Product life extension**: Designing goods for durability, repair, and reuse prevents unnecessary disposal.
- **Biodegradable alternatives**: Using compostable packaging, bio-based plastics, and natural fibers ensures that products break down safely in the environment.
- **Circular water systems**: Treating and recycling wastewater prevents chemical pollution in rivers and oceans.

By eliminating pollution sources, circular solutions help restore degraded environments and improve air, soil, and water quality.

Enhancing Biodiversity and Habitat Restoration

Biodiversity loss is directly linked to habitat destruction, pollution, and climate change—all consequences of unsustainable economic practices. Circularity supports biodiversity conservation by ensuring that natural habitats remain functioning, resilient ecosystems.

Circular Strategies for Biodiversity Protection:

- **Rewilding and land reclamation**: Abandoned or degraded lands are restored into forests, wetlands, or grasslands using nature-based solutions.
- **Agroecological farming**: Sustainable agriculture techniques, such as crop rotation, agroforestry, and regenerative grazing, enhance soil health and support diverse ecosystems.
- **Sustainable fisheries and marine restoration**: Circular seafood supply chains ensure that fishing practices do not deplete marine populations or harm fragile ecosystems.
- **Urban biodiversity initiatives**: Green roofs, living walls, and wildlife corridors integrate nature into urban areas, reducing habitat fragmentation.

By aligning economic systems with ecological cycles, circular models help protect species diversity and ecological balance.

Strengthening Climate Resilience Through Circular Strategies

Climate change is one of the most pressing ecological threats, causing rising temperatures, extreme weather events, and shifting ecosystems. The circular economy contributes to climate resilience by reducing carbon footprints, optimizing resource efficiency, and promoting low-impact industries.

Circular Approaches for Climate Resilience:

- **Carbon sequestration through circular agriculture**: Regenerative practices, such as no-till farming and soil carbon capture, help absorb atmospheric CO_2.
- **Renewable energy adoption**: Circular systems prioritize solar, wind, and bio-based energy to replace fossil fuels.

- **Closed-loop manufacturing**: Producing goods with recycled materials significantly lowers greenhouse gas emissions.
- **Sustainable urban planning**: Circular infrastructure designs focus on energy-efficient buildings, smart grids, and public transport, reducing urban carbon footprints.

By integrating circular practices into economic and environmental policies, societies can adapt to and mitigate climate change, protecting both ecosystems and human communities.

Challenges and Opportunities in Circular Ecosystem Restoration

The integration of circular economy principles into ecosystem restoration presents both challenges and opportunities. While circular approaches offer long-term solutions to environmental degradation, their implementation requires overcoming technical, financial, regulatory, and societal barriers. At the same time, advancements in policy, technology, and public awareness are creating new opportunities to scale up circular ecosystem restoration.

This section explores the key challenges hindering circular restoration efforts and the opportunities that can drive their widespread adoption and success.

Key Challenges in Circular Ecosystem Restoration

Despite the potential benefits, several challenges must be addressed for circular economy principles to be effectively integrated into ecosystem restoration efforts.

Lack of Infrastructure and Technology for Circular Systems

Many regions still rely on linear economic models, where waste disposal, resource extraction, and pollution are not managed within a closed-loop system. The transition to circular restoration practices requires:

- Investment in recycling and resource recovery facilities to support material reuse in ecosystem restoration.
- Improved waste management systems, particularly in developing regions, to reduce environmental contamination.
- Advanced monitoring technologies to track the impact of circular restoration projects.

Without the proper infrastructure, circular approaches can be difficult to implement on a large scale.

Financial and Economic Barriers

Circular restoration often requires upfront investment in sustainable materials, regenerative practices, and research. Challenges include:

- High initial costs associated with bio-based materials, renewable energy, and waste processing technologies.
- Limited funding and incentives for circular projects, particularly in countries with weak environmental policies.
- Market resistance, as some industries prioritize short-term profits over long-term sustainability.

To overcome these financial obstacles, governments and businesses must work together to support funding mechanisms for circular ecosystem restoration.

Regulatory and Policy Gaps

Many environmental policies and regulations are designed around traditional waste disposal and resource extraction practices, creating barriers for circular economy adoption.

- Rigid permitting processes may slow down the implementation of nature-based restoration projects.
- Lack of standardization in circular materials and processes may discourage businesses from investing in sustainable alternatives.
- Insufficient enforcement of waste reduction policies allows pollution and ecosystem degradation to continue.

Aligning regulatory frameworks with circular principles will be necessary to facilitate widespread adoption.

Public Awareness and Behavioral Change

Transitioning to circular restoration requires cultural and behavioral shifts among individuals, businesses, and policymakers. Challenges include:

- Limited understanding of circular economy benefits among the general public.
- Resistance to change in industries accustomed to linear economic models.
- Lack of engagement in sustainable practices, such as composting, recycling, and regenerative land use.

Education and advocacy are critical to promoting circular thinking and community-driven restoration efforts.

Opportunities for Advancing Circular Ecosystem Restoration

While challenges exist, there are significant opportunities to expand and improve circular ecosystem restoration efforts.

Advancements in Circular and Regenerative Technologies

Innovation in biotechnology, material science, and artificial intelligence is driving more efficient circular solutions. Opportunities include:

- Bio-based materials for restoration, such as biodegradable erosion control products and sustainable construction materials.
- AI-driven resource optimization, helping cities and industries reduce waste and improve efficiency.
- Water purification and recycling innovations, enhancing water availability in degraded environments.

Technological advancements will play a key role in scaling up circular restoration strategies.

Growth of Policy and Market Incentives

Governments and industries are increasingly recognizing the value of circular economy strategies, leading to:

- Tax incentives and subsidies for businesses adopting circular restoration practices.
- Extended producer responsibility (EPR) programs, requiring manufacturers to design products with reuse and recyclability in mind.
- Carbon credit markets, where companies investing in circular ecosystem restoration can receive financial benefits.

With stronger policy support, circular restoration can become economically viable and widely implemented.

Business and Investment Opportunities in Circular Restoration

A shift toward green investment and sustainable finance is creating new business models that support circular ecosystem restoration. Opportunities include:

- Impact investing in circular projects, where investors seek both environmental and financial returns.
- Development of circular supply chains, reducing dependency on virgin resources and increasing material efficiency.
- Public-private partnerships, allowing businesses and governments to collaborate on large-scale restoration initiatives.

With growing interest in corporate sustainability and ESG (Environmental, Social, and Governance) reporting, circular restoration is gaining momentum.

Community Engagement and Circular Economy Education

Building public awareness and community participation can help integrate circular principles into daily practices and local restoration efforts. Opportunities include:

- Educational programs on waste reduction and resource efficiency, empowering individuals to take action.
- Citizen-led restoration projects, such as community tree planting and urban composting programs.
- Collaborations between businesses, NGOs, and governments, fostering circular initiatives at multiple levels.

By engaging communities and fostering knowledge-sharing, circular restoration efforts can be scaled more effectively.

Chapter 2: Resource Efficiency and Regenerative Practices

The overextraction of natural resources and inefficient use of materials have led to widespread environmental degradation, habitat loss, and ecosystem instability. Traditional economic models prioritize short-term productivity over long-term sustainability, resulting in deforestation, soil depletion, water scarcity, and excessive waste generation. These practices have placed immense pressure on ecosystems, reducing their ability to recover naturally.

A circular economy approach emphasizes resource efficiency by maximizing the use of existing materials, reducing waste, and designing products and systems for durability and reuse. At the same time, regenerative practices focus on restoring natural cycles by enhancing soil health, increasing biodiversity, and improving water retention. Together, these approaches help ensure that ecosystems can recover, sustain biodiversity, and continue providing essential services.

This chapter explores how resource efficiency and regenerative strategies contribute to ecosystem restoration. It examines the importance of reducing resource extraction through circular models, enhancing ecosystems through regenerative design, implementing closed-loop systems, and restoring natural cycles. By adopting these approaches, businesses, governments, and communities can minimize their ecological footprint while actively contributing to long-term environmental resilience.

Reducing Resource Extraction Through Circular Models

The extraction of raw materials, such as minerals, fossil fuels, timber, and water, places immense pressure on ecosystems, leading to deforestation, soil degradation, habitat destruction, and biodiversity loss. Traditional economic models operate on a linear approach—resources are extracted, processed, used, and discarded—creating a system that is resource-intensive and environmentally unsustainable.

A circular economy model aims to reduce the demand for raw materials by keeping resources in use for as long as possible through reuse, recycling, refurbishment, and regenerative practices. By transitioning from a resource-extractive economy to one that maximizes resource efficiency, societies can minimize environmental damage while meeting economic needs.

This section explores how circular models help reduce resource extraction by focusing on material efficiency, industrial symbiosis, sustainable product design, and regenerative resource use.

Improving Material Efficiency and Waste Reduction

One of the most effective ways to reduce resource extraction is to use fewer raw materials while maximizing the efficiency of existing resources. Many industries rely on high levels of material waste due to inefficient production and disposal methods. Circular models address this issue by focusing on waste reduction, material optimization, and closed-loop production cycles.

Circular Strategies for Material Efficiency:

- **Lightweighting products**: Designing materials to be lighter yet stronger to reduce raw material consumption.
- **Precision manufacturing**: Using advanced technology (e.g., 3D printing, AI-driven production) to minimize material waste during fabrication.
- **Lean production techniques**: Eliminating excess resource use through optimized supply chain and production processes.

By improving material efficiency, industries can reduce the need for continuous resource extraction, thereby lowering environmental degradation and energy consumption.

Industrial Symbiosis: Sharing Resources Between Industries

Industries traditionally function in isolated supply chains, where waste generated by one sector is discarded rather than repurposed. Industrial symbiosis promotes cross-industry resource sharing, where waste or byproducts from one industry become valuable inputs for another. This model reduces the demand for new raw materials while simultaneously lowering waste production.

Examples of Industrial Symbiosis:

- **Heat and energy recovery**: Factories can capture excess heat from manufacturing and redirect it to nearby residential or agricultural areas.
- **Reusing industrial byproducts**: Waste materials from steel, cement, or agriculture can be transformed into raw materials for construction, biofuels, or textiles.
- **Circular water management**: Industries can treat and recycle wastewater rather than extracting freshwater from natural sources.

Industrial symbiosis ensures that materials remain in circulation longer, reducing the need for new extraction while lowering waste generation and energy use.

Sustainable Product Design and Circular Innovation

Many products are designed for single-use consumption, contributing to rapid depletion of resources and high levels of waste. Circular economy models emphasize designing products for longevity, repairability, and recyclability, reducing the demand for new materials.

Circular Product Design Strategies:

- **Modular product design**: Creating products with interchangeable parts that can be easily repaired or upgraded.
- **Cradle-to-cradle manufacturing**: Designing products that are fully recyclable or biodegradable, ensuring they do not contribute to landfill waste.
- **Material substitution**: Replacing finite resources with renewable, bio-based, or recycled alternatives (e.g., using bamboo instead of hardwood, or recycled metals instead of virgin ore).

Sustainable product design reduces the need for continued resource extraction by ensuring that materials stay in use longer and can be reintroduced into production cycles.

Regenerative Resource Use and Eco-Friendly Alternatives

Beyond reducing extraction, circular models also focus on regenerating natural resources through sustainable practices. By integrating nature-based solutions and regenerative approaches, ecosystems can recover from resource-intensive activities while continuing to provide essential services.

Key Regenerative Strategies:

- **Sustainable forestry**: Implementing selective logging, reforestation, and agroforestry to maintain forest ecosystems while still meeting timber demands.
- **Regenerative agriculture**: Using cover crops, crop rotation, and no-till farming to restore soil fertility, reducing the need for synthetic fertilizers and excessive land use.
- **Eco-friendly materials**: Promoting bio-based plastics, plant-based textiles, and biodegradable packaging to reduce dependency on petroleum-based resources.

By adopting regenerative practices, industries and communities can restore natural ecosystems while ensuring a continuous, sustainable supply of materials.

Enhancing Ecosystems Through Regenerative Design

Traditional development and land use practices have often prioritized short-term resource extraction and infrastructure expansion, leading to ecosystem degradation, biodiversity loss, and declining soil and water quality. Conventional restoration efforts focus on damage control, but they do not always ensure long-term ecosystem resilience. Regenerative design goes beyond restoration by actively enhancing ecosystems, ensuring they become more resilient, productive, and capable of self-renewal over time.

Regenerative design aligns with circular economy principles by integrating nature-based solutions, closed-loop systems, and adaptive land management strategies to restore and strengthen natural environments. This approach does not just repair damage; it enhances ecosystem functions, improves biodiversity, and creates sustainable landscapes that support both nature and human well-being.

This section explores how regenerative design enhances ecosystems by focusing on nature-based restoration, regenerative land-use strategies, biodiversity-centered design, and climate-resilient landscapes.

Nature-Based Solutions for Ecosystem Enhancement

Nature-based solutions (NbS) leverage natural processes to restore degraded ecosystems while providing long-term environmental, social, and economic benefits. These solutions integrate ecological knowledge with sustainable development, ensuring that human activities work in harmony with nature.

Key Nature-Based Solutions in Regenerative Design:

- **Wetland restoration**: Revitalizing degraded wetlands to enhance water filtration, flood protection, and biodiversity.
- **Reforestation and afforestation**: Planting native trees to restore carbon sequestration, improve air quality, and regulate local climates.
- **Soil regeneration through organic amendments**: Using compost, biochar, and microbial inoculants to rebuild soil health and increase agricultural productivity.
- **Coastal and marine ecosystem rehabilitation**: Restoring mangroves, coral reefs, and seagrass meadows to protect shorelines and enhance marine biodiversity.

By implementing nature-based solutions, ecosystems are enhanced rather than merely repaired, allowing them to regenerate and thrive over time.

Regenerative Land-Use Strategies

Conventional land-use practices have led to deforestation, soil depletion, and habitat fragmentation. Regenerative land-use strategies aim to restore degraded lands while ensuring they continue to support agriculture, forestry, and urban development in a sustainable way.

Circular Approaches to Regenerative Land Use:

- **Agroforestry**: Combining tree cultivation with agriculture to enhance soil fertility, reduce erosion, and increase biodiversity.
- **Regenerative grazing**: Implementing rotational grazing to prevent overgrazing and allow pasture ecosystems to recover naturally.
- **Urban greening**: Integrating green roofs, living walls, and community gardens to improve biodiversity in urban environments.

- **Land reclamation through permaculture**: Designing landscapes based on natural ecosystems to enhance soil health, water retention, and plant diversity.

By shifting to regenerative land-use models, degraded landscapes can be restored to full ecological function, increasing their ability to support both nature and human communities.

Biodiversity-Centered Design for Resilient Ecosystems

Biodiversity is essential for healthy and functional ecosystems, but habitat destruction, pollution, and climate change have contributed to species decline and ecosystem imbalance. Regenerative design focuses on enhancing biodiversity by creating self-sustaining ecosystems where species can thrive.

Strategies for Biodiversity-Centered Regeneration:

- **Habitat corridors**: Connecting fragmented ecosystems with wildlife corridors and green infrastructure to support species migration and genetic diversity.
- **Native species reintroduction**: Restoring pollinators, keystone species, and endemic plants to rebuild ecosystem balance.
- **Microhabitat restoration**: Creating small-scale refuges, such as pollinator gardens and urban wetlands, to enhance local biodiversity.
- **Soil microbiome enrichment**: Supporting soil bacteria, fungi, and invertebrates that promote plant health and carbon storage.

By designing ecosystems with biodiversity in mind, regenerative strategies help restore ecological balance, ensuring that ecosystems remain productive and resilient in the long term.

Climate-Resilient Landscapes and Adaptive Design

Climate change poses a significant challenge to ecosystem stability, increasing the frequency of extreme weather events, droughts, and habitat loss. Regenerative design ensures that ecosystems are not only restored but also resilient to future environmental changes.

Key Climate-Resilient Regenerative Strategies:

- **Water-sensitive urban design (WSUD)**: Using permeable pavements, rain gardens, and green infrastructure to manage urban flooding and reduce heat stress.
- **Drought-resistant agriculture**: Implementing rainwater harvesting, drought-resistant crops, and soil moisture retention techniques to support food production in arid regions.
- **Coastal resilience projects**: Restoring dunes, wetlands, and mangrove forests to buffer against sea-level rise and storm surges.
- **Carbon-sequestering landscapes**: Enhancing carbon sinks through reforestation, regenerative farming, and soil restoration to mitigate climate change impacts.

By integrating climate resilience into regenerative design, ecosystems become better equipped to withstand future disruptions, ensuring long-term environmental and economic stability.

The Role of Closed-Loop Systems in Reducing Environmental Impact

The traditional linear economy follows a take-make-dispose model, where resources are extracted, used, and discarded as waste. This system has contributed to widespread pollution, resource depletion, and environmental degradation. In contrast, closed-loop systems prioritize continuous resource circulation, ensuring that materials, energy, and nutrients are efficiently reused, repurposed, or regenerated.

By eliminating waste and keeping materials in circulation for as long as possible, closed-loop systems reduce environmental impact, lower resource extraction rates, and enhance ecosystem resilience. This approach is integral to the circular economy and plays a critical role in ecosystem restoration and climate adaptation.

This section explores how closed-loop systems contribute to waste reduction, resource efficiency, industrial sustainability, and ecosystem regeneration.

Waste Reduction Through Closed-Loop Resource Cycles

Waste generation is a major driver of landfill accumulation, air and water pollution, and habitat destruction. In closed-loop systems, waste is eliminated at the source by ensuring that all byproducts and discarded materials are recycled, upcycled, or repurposed.

Key Strategies for Waste Reduction in Closed-Loop Systems:

- **Material recovery and recycling**: Capturing valuable materials from discarded products and reintroducing them into manufacturing cycles (e.g., recycling plastics, metals, and glass).
- **Industrial byproduct utilization**: Waste from one industrial process becomes a resource for another, reducing raw material extraction.
- **Organic waste composting and bio-conversion**: Food and agricultural waste can be converted into fertilizers, biofuels, and animal feed, rather than contributing to methane emissions in landfills.
- **Waste-to-energy technologies**: Capturing methane from landfills and anaerobic digesters to generate renewable energy.

By redefining waste as a resource, closed-loop systems contribute to cleaner environments, lower emissions, and more sustainable material flows.

Increasing Resource Efficiency in Industrial Processes

Industries are some of the largest consumers of natural resources, including water, energy, and raw materials. Closed-loop systems help industries optimize resource use, reduce inefficiencies, and minimize environmental impact.

Examples of Resource Efficiency Through Closed-Loop Systems:

- **Water recycling and reuse**: Industries and municipalities can implement wastewater treatment and rainwater harvesting to reduce dependency on freshwater sources.
- **Circular manufacturing**: Factories can incorporate remanufacturing and refurbishment to extend product life cycles and minimize waste.
- **Smart material use**: Lightweighting materials, 3D printing, and precision manufacturing reduce excess resource consumption while maintaining product durability.
- **Energy-efficient production cycles**: Capturing waste heat from industrial processes and repurposing it for heating, cooling, or electricity generation.

By integrating closed-loop systems into industrial processes, resource extraction is reduced, and ecosystems are less burdened by pollution and excessive consumption.

Supporting Sustainable Agriculture and Land Restoration

Agriculture is a major contributor to deforestation, soil degradation, and water depletion, but closed-loop farming techniques help restore ecosystems while maintaining food security.

Closed-Loop Approaches in Agriculture:

- **Regenerative farming**: Crop residues and livestock manure are composted and returned to the soil, enhancing fertility and reducing synthetic fertilizer use.
- **Agroforestry and intercropping**: Planting trees alongside crops enhances biodiversity, reduces erosion, and improves soil moisture retention.
- **Closed-loop water systems**: Irrigation runoff is captured, filtered, and reused, minimizing water waste and preventing chemical contamination of natural waterways.
- **Circular livestock systems**: Integrating livestock with crop production allows for natural nutrient cycling, reducing reliance on external inputs.

By implementing closed-loop agricultural models, ecosystems can recover from overgrazing, soil depletion, and excessive chemical use, leading to long-term sustainability.

Ecosystem Regeneration and Climate Resilience

Closed-loop systems contribute to ecosystem restoration by ensuring that natural resources are regenerated rather than depleted. These models help ecosystems recover from deforestation, pollution, and climate-related disturbances.

Key Strategies for Closed-Loop Ecosystem Restoration:

- **Circular forestry management**: Replanting native tree species after timber harvesting and using wood waste for biodegradable products and bioenergy.
- **Blue economy innovations**: Restoring marine ecosystems through closed-loop aquaculture, oyster reef restoration, and seaweed farming.
- **Carbon sequestration through soil regeneration**: Capturing carbon in soil organic matter and reforested landscapes to combat climate change.
- **Biodiversity conservation in closed-loop urban planning**: Designing cities with green roofs, rain gardens, and

permeable pavements to reduce flooding and increase biodiversity.

By using closed-loop strategies for land and water restoration, ecosystems become more resilient to environmental pressures and climate change impacts.

Restoring Natural Cycles Through Circular Resource Use

Natural ecosystems operate in closed-loop cycles, where materials and energy are continuously reused, supporting biodiversity, nutrient cycling, and environmental stability. However, human activities— such as deforestation, industrial pollution, overextraction of resources, and excessive waste production—have disrupted these cycles, leading to climate change, soil degradation, water scarcity, and biodiversity loss.

The circular economy seeks to restore natural cycles by ensuring that resources are used efficiently, regenerated, and reintegrated into ecosystems without harm. By aligning human activities with nature's regenerative processes, circular resource use helps restore ecosystems, enhance climate resilience, and create long-term environmental sustainability.

This section explores how circular strategies can help restore natural water cycles, nutrient cycles, carbon cycles, and biodiversity regeneration processes, ensuring a balanced, self-sustaining environment.

Restoring the Water Cycle Through Circular Water Management

Water is a finite resource, yet human activities disrupt the natural hydrological cycle through overuse, pollution, and inefficient management. Circular water use ensures that water is conserved, reused, and purified naturally, preventing depletion and contamination.

Circular Strategies for Water Cycle Restoration:

- **Rainwater harvesting and groundwater recharge**: Capturing and storing rainwater for irrigation and urban use reduces dependency on freshwater sources and helps replenish groundwater.
- **Nature-based water purification**: Wetlands, constructed wetlands, and riparian buffer zones naturally filter pollutants, restoring clean water ecosystems.
- **Water recycling and closed-loop wastewater treatment**: Treating and reusing wastewater in agriculture, industry, and urban systems reduces freshwater withdrawal and minimizes pollution.
- **Sustainable agricultural water use**: Drip irrigation, precision farming, and agroforestry improve water retention in soils, reducing excessive water consumption.

By applying circular water management, societies can restore natural hydrological cycles, protect freshwater ecosystems, and ensure long-term water availability.

Closing Nutrient Loops to Restore Soil Health

Soils play a critical role in food production, carbon sequestration, and water retention, but conventional farming depletes nutrients and organic matter, leading to soil degradation and desertification. Circular agriculture focuses on restoring soil fertility through closed-loop nutrient management.

Key Circular Strategies for Soil Regeneration:

- **Composting organic waste**: Food scraps, crop residues, and livestock manure can be composted and returned to the soil, enriching its nutrient content.

- **Regenerative farming techniques**: Cover cropping, crop rotation, and reduced tillage help maintain soil structure, microbial activity, and nutrient levels.
- **Biochar and organic amendments**: Applying biochar (charcoal produced from organic waste) improves soil fertility and increases carbon sequestration.
- **Circular livestock systems**: Integrating grazing animals with crop production ensures that nutrients are naturally cycled between plants and animals.

By restoring nutrient loops, circular agriculture prevents soil degradation, reduces reliance on synthetic fertilizers, and enhances ecosystem health.

Regenerating Carbon Cycles Through Circular Economy Practices

The carbon cycle regulates Earth's climate by storing and cycling carbon through the atmosphere, plants, oceans, and soil. However, deforestation, fossil fuel combustion, and industrial pollution have disrupted this cycle, increasing carbon emissions and global temperatures. Circular practices help restore natural carbon sequestration by promoting low-carbon alternatives and carbon-storing landscapes.

Circular Strategies for Carbon Cycle Restoration:

- **Carbon sequestration in forests and soils**: Reforestation, agroforestry, and regenerative farming enhance carbon absorption, reducing atmospheric CO_2.
- **Bio-based materials and green construction**: Using plant-based materials, such as bamboo and hempcrete, stores carbon naturally while reducing fossil fuel use.
- **Waste-to-energy and bioenergy solutions**: Capturing methane from organic waste decomposition prevents greenhouse gas emissions and provides renewable energy.

- **Circular urban planning**: Expanding green roofs, urban forests, and carbon-neutral cities lowers overall carbon footprints.

By restoring the carbon cycle, circular strategies contribute to climate change mitigation and long-term environmental stability.

Enhancing Biodiversity Through Circular Ecosystem Regeneration

Biodiversity is essential for ecosystem balance, food security, and climate adaptation, yet habitat destruction, pollution, and unsustainable land use have accelerated species decline and ecosystem collapse. Circular resource use ensures that biodiversity is protected and ecosystems remain functional.

Circular Strategies for Biodiversity Restoration:

- **Rewilding and habitat connectivity**: Restoring degraded landscapes and creating wildlife corridors reconnects fragmented habitats, supporting species migration and reproduction.
- **Sustainable fisheries and marine conservation**: Implementing circular seafood supply chains, marine protected areas, and seaweed farming preserves ocean biodiversity.
- **Urban biodiversity initiatives**: Integrating pollinator gardens, green spaces, and water-sensitive landscaping in cities supports native species.
- **Eliminating pollution through circular material use**: Reducing plastic waste, toxic runoff, and synthetic chemicals prevents ecosystem contamination, protecting wildlife.

By closing resource loops in biodiversity management, ecosystems can recover naturally and sustainably, ensuring long-term ecological balance.

Chapter 3: Waste Management and Pollution Reduction

Waste generation and pollution are among the most pressing environmental challenges, contributing to land degradation, water contamination, air pollution, and biodiversity loss. The traditional linear economy, based on a take-make-dispose model, has led to overfilled landfills, plastic pollution in oceans, and toxic emissions from industries and households. Without intervention, these issues will continue to harm ecosystems, disrupt natural cycles, and threaten human health.

A circular economy approach to waste management and pollution reduction aims to eliminate waste at the source, repurpose materials, and reduce environmental harm. By designing out waste, promoting material recovery, and adopting cleaner production methods, industries and communities can minimize pollution while ensuring that resources remain in circulation for as long as possible.

This chapter explores circular strategies for minimizing waste and pollution, restoring ecosystems affected by contamination, turning waste into valuable resources, and advancing innovations in circular waste management. By transitioning to waste-free and low-pollution systems, societies can create cleaner environments while supporting long-term sustainability goals.

Circular Strategies for Minimizing Waste and Pollution

The linear economy—where resources are extracted, used, and discarded—has led to unmanageable waste levels and severe environmental pollution. Landfills overflow with non-biodegradable materials, waterways are contaminated with industrial and plastic waste, and air pollution from manufacturing and transportation contributes to climate change and public health concerns. These environmental pressures require a shift to circular waste management strategies that focus on waste prevention, resource recovery, and pollution reduction.

The circular economy aims to eliminate waste at its source, keeping materials and products in use for as long as possible. Through innovative design, efficient waste processing, and responsible consumption, circular strategies help minimize pollution while reducing the demand for virgin resources.

This section explores four key circular strategies for minimizing waste and pollution: waste prevention, material recovery, industrial symbiosis, and biodegradable alternatives.

Waste Prevention Through Circular Design

The most effective way to minimize waste is to prevent it from being created in the first place. Circular design principles focus on creating products and systems that reduce material use, extend product life cycles, and eliminate unnecessary waste.

Key Approaches to Circular Waste Prevention:

- **Eco-design and product durability**: Designing products for long-term use, easy repair, and modular upgrades reduces waste by preventing premature disposal.
- **Lightweighting materials**: Using stronger yet lighter materials minimizes resource consumption while maintaining product quality.
- **Minimizing packaging waste**: Shifting to reusable, compostable, or minimal packaging reduces single-use plastic waste.
- **Closed-loop supply chains**: Manufacturers use remanufactured or refurbished components to reduce the need for raw materials.

By integrating waste reduction into product design, industries and businesses can prevent unnecessary pollution while optimizing resource efficiency.

Maximizing Material Recovery and Recycling

Recycling and material recovery play a crucial role in keeping valuable resources in circulation rather than allowing them to end up in landfills or incinerators. Effective material recovery reduces pollution, conserves natural resources, and lowers energy consumption compared to virgin material extraction.

Strategies for Enhancing Material Recovery:

- **Advanced sorting and recycling technologies**: Automated sorting systems and AI-driven waste management improve the efficiency of recycling facilities.
- **Design for disassembly**: Products designed for easy separation of components make material recovery and recycling more effective.
- **Decentralized waste collection systems**: Community-based recycling initiatives encourage higher participation in circular waste management.
- **Chemical and biological recycling innovations**: Emerging technologies allow for plastic depolymerization, organic waste bio-conversion, and textile recycling.

A well-functioning recycling and material recovery system ensures that waste is not just diverted from disposal but also reintegrated into the economy in a sustainable, efficient manner.

Industrial Symbiosis: Turning Waste into Resources

Industrial waste is a significant contributor to pollution, but industrial symbiosis creates opportunities to reuse waste materials between industries, reducing overall waste generation. By exchanging byproducts, heat, and energy, industries can repurpose waste into new materials or energy sources.

Circular Industrial Waste Management Strategies:

- **Using industrial byproducts in construction**: Fly ash, slag, and recycled concrete can be used in road building and infrastructure projects.
- **Waste-to-energy conversion**: Organic waste and residual biomass can be used for biogas, biofuels, and heat recovery.
- **Cross-sectoral resource exchange**: Factories in the same region can establish waste-sharing networks, where one facility's waste becomes another's input material.
- **Water reuse in industrial processes**: Recycling wastewater for cooling, processing, and irrigation reduces the need for freshwater extraction.

Industrial symbiosis minimizes waste disposal costs, lowers emissions, and enhances sustainability across multiple industries.

Shifting to Biodegradable and Non-Toxic Alternatives

Many waste and pollution problems arise from non-biodegradable materials that persist in the environment for decades. Circular strategies promote the transition to biodegradable, compostable, and non-toxic materials to replace harmful plastics, chemicals, and synthetic compounds.

Innovations in Sustainable Materials:

- **Biodegradable plastics and biopolymers**: Made from plant-based sources like corn, seaweed, and sugarcane, these alternatives break down naturally without harming ecosystems.

- **Compostable packaging**: Packaging made from mushrooms, bamboo fibers, and agricultural waste decomposes safely in soil or composting facilities.
- **Natural fiber textiles**: Using hemp, bamboo, and organic cotton instead of synthetic fibers prevents microplastic pollution in waterways.
- **Non-toxic, circular chemistry**: Developing green alternatives to industrial chemicals reduces hazardous waste production and soil contamination.

By replacing non-renewable and pollutive materials with circular alternatives, industries can significantly reduce long-term waste accumulation and environmental toxicity.

Restoring Ecosystems Affected by Waste and Contamination

Human activities have significantly impacted ecosystems through pollution, improper waste disposal, and industrial contamination, leading to land degradation, water pollution, and loss of biodiversity. Traditional waste management systems often focus on removal or containment, but these methods do not always address the long-term consequences of contamination. A circular approach to ecosystem restoration seeks to clean, regenerate, and integrate waste into sustainable resource cycles, ensuring that damaged environments are rehabilitated and protected from further harm.

This section explores key strategies for restoring ecosystems affected by waste and contamination, including bioremediation, circular land rehabilitation, water system restoration, and pollution prevention through circular waste management.

Bioremediation: Using Nature to Clean Polluted Environments

Bioremediation is a nature-based solution that utilizes microorganisms, plants, and fungi to remove pollutants from soil, water, and air. It is a cost-effective and environmentally friendly method for decontaminating ecosystems without causing further harm.

Key Bioremediation Techniques:

- **Phytoremediation**: Using plants to absorb and break down pollutants in soil and water. Certain species, such as sunflowers and willows, can remove heavy metals and toxins from contaminated areas.
- **Mycoremediation**: Fungi, particularly mycelium networks, break down petroleum-based pollutants, pesticides, and industrial chemicals, restoring soil and water quality.
- **Microbial degradation**: Bacteria and other microorganisms help neutralize hazardous chemicals, such as oil spills or heavy metal contamination in water sources.
- **Wetland restoration**: Constructed wetlands filter contaminants from stormwater runoff, industrial wastewater, and agricultural pollutants, improving water quality.

By harnessing biological processes, bioremediation helps ecosystems self-cleanse and regenerate, reducing the long-term impact of contamination.

Circular Land Rehabilitation: Restoring Contaminated Soils and Degraded Land

Industrial waste, mining, and agricultural runoff contribute to soil contamination and degradation, making land unsuitable for agriculture, forestry, or natural ecosystems. Circular land rehabilitation ensures that polluted and degraded lands are restored to productive use through sustainable remediation techniques.

Circular Strategies for Land Rehabilitation:

- **Soil amendment with organic matter**: Compost, biochar, and green manure improve soil fertility and restore microbial balance in contaminated areas.

- **Reforestation and afforestation**: Planting native species on degraded land helps rebuild soil stability, increase biodiversity, and sequester carbon.
- **Sustainable mine reclamation**: Former mining sites can be replanted with vegetation, repurposed for renewable energy projects, or transformed into wetland ecosystems.
- **Erosion control through natural barriers**: Planting grasses, shrubs, and trees prevents soil loss and helps rebuild degraded landscapes.

Circular rehabilitation techniques restore soil health, promote biodiversity, and allow previously contaminated land to be reintegrated into natural and economic systems.

Restoring Water Systems Affected by Pollution and Waste

Water bodies are highly vulnerable to industrial discharge, plastic pollution, and chemical runoff, leading to ecosystem imbalances, loss of aquatic biodiversity, and health risks for human populations. Restoring contaminated water systems requires circular water management strategies that remove pollutants while ensuring long-term water sustainability.

Circular Approaches for Water Restoration:

- **Floating wetlands and biofiltration**: Artificial wetlands and aquatic plants help filter nutrients, heavy metals, and chemicals from polluted rivers and lakes.
- **Plastic waste recovery and recycling**: Removing microplastics and floating debris from oceans and waterways ensures that marine life is protected from further contamination.
- **Sustainable wastewater treatment and reuse**: Treating industrial and municipal wastewater for reuse in agriculture, industry, and urban areas reduces reliance on freshwater sources.

- **Regenerative coastal and riverbank restoration**: Restoring mangroves, seagrass meadows, and riverbanks enhances natural filtration systems and prevents further erosion.

By integrating nature-based water purification and circular waste recovery, polluted water ecosystems can be revitalized and protected from future contamination.

Pollution Prevention Through Circular Waste Management

Restoring ecosystems alone is not enough—preventing future contamination is essential for long-term environmental sustainability. Circular waste management ensures that waste materials are continuously repurposed, eliminating the need for landfill disposal and pollution-intensive production methods.

Strategies for Pollution Prevention in Circular Systems:

- **Zero-waste manufacturing**: Industries design production processes that eliminate waste and reuse materials, preventing industrial pollution.
- **EPR**: Companies are held accountable for the full lifecycle of their products, encouraging recyclable and repairable product design.
- **Decentralized composting and bio-waste conversion**: Organic waste is transformed into fertilizer, biogas, or soil amendments, reducing landfill dependency.
- **Circular plastic economy**: Reducing plastic production, increasing biodegradable alternatives, and improving global recycling infrastructure limit plastic pollution in marine and terrestrial ecosystems.

By addressing waste at the source, pollution prevention strategies ensure that restored ecosystems remain healthy and resilient.

Turning Waste into a Resource: Industrial and Biological Waste Valorization

Waste is often seen as an environmental burden, contributing to pollution, land degradation, and resource depletion. However, in a circular economy, waste is not an endpoint—it is a valuable resource that can be repurposed, transformed, and reintegrated into productive use. Waste valorization, the process of converting industrial and biological waste into useful products, plays a crucial role in reducing environmental impact while creating economic and environmental benefits.

By shifting away from traditional waste disposal methods, such as landfilling and incineration, waste valorization supports sustainable industrial processes, resource efficiency, and environmental restoration. This section explores circular strategies for repurposing industrial waste, utilizing organic waste for energy and agriculture, promoting bio-based materials, and integrating waste-to-energy solutions.

Industrial Waste Repurposing and Material Recovery

Industries generate vast amounts of waste, including metal scraps, chemicals, construction debris, and electronic waste (e-waste). Traditionally, much of this waste has been discarded in landfills or incinerated, contributing to air and water pollution. Waste valorization focuses on recovering, refining, and reusing industrial byproducts, extending the lifecycle of materials while reducing the need for raw resource extraction.

Strategies for Industrial Waste Valorization:

- **Recycling metals and electronic waste**: Metals from discarded electronics, machinery, and appliances can be extracted, purified, and reused in new manufacturing processes.
- **Construction waste repurposing**: Crushed concrete and reclaimed bricks can be reused in infrastructure projects, reducing demand for new building materials.

45

- **Chemical and solvent recovery**: Industries can reclaim and purify solvents, acids, and other chemicals for reuse, reducing hazardous waste disposal.
- **Industrial symbiosis**: Waste from one industry can become a raw material for another (e.g., using steel manufacturing byproducts in cement production).

By maximizing waste recovery and reuse, industries can reduce production costs, lower environmental impact, and promote a circular industrial economy.

Biological Waste Valorization for Agriculture and Food Systems

Organic waste, including food scraps, crop residues, and livestock manure, often ends up in landfills, where it decomposes and emits methane—a potent greenhouse gas. However, biological waste can be repurposed into valuable products that support agriculture, improve soil health, and reduce the need for synthetic fertilizers.

Circular Solutions for Organic Waste Valorization:

- **Composting and soil enrichment**: Organic waste is converted into nutrient-rich compost, enhancing soil fertility while reducing landfill waste.
- **Biochar production**: Agricultural residues can be processed into biochar, a carbon-rich material that improves soil structure and retains nutrients.
- **Livestock feed from food waste**: Safe and regulated food waste can be processed into feed for animals, reducing reliance on conventional feed crops.
- **Fertilizer production from organic byproducts**: Nutrient-rich waste streams from food processing can be converted into liquid and solid organic fertilizers.

By using biological waste as a resource for agriculture, food systems become more sustainable and circular, reducing environmental pressures while supporting soil regeneration and climate resilience.

Bio-Based Materials and Alternative Product Development

Plastics, synthetic fibers, and petroleum-based materials contribute to long-term pollution and environmental damage. Waste valorization allows for the development of bio-based alternatives derived from agricultural and industrial byproducts.

Innovations in Bio-Based Waste Valorization:

- **Plant-based plastics**: Starch, seaweed, and agricultural residues can be used to produce biodegradable packaging and bio-based plastics.
- **Textile fibers from agricultural waste**: Fibers from pineapple leaves, hemp, and coconut husks can replace synthetic fabrics in clothing and textiles.
- **Paper and packaging from agricultural residues**: Sugarcane bagasse, wheat straw, and corn husks can be processed into eco-friendly paper products.
- **Biopolymers and adhesives**: Agricultural waste byproducts can be used in sustainable adhesives, coatings, and biodegradable polymers.

By transforming waste into valuable materials, industries can reduce dependency on finite resources while creating sustainable consumer products.

Waste-to-Energy Solutions for Sustainable Resource Use

Not all waste can be recycled into new materials, but waste-to-energy (WTE) technologies ensure that even non-recyclable waste can contribute to a sustainable energy system. These solutions reduce landfill dependency while generating renewable energy for electricity, heating, and industrial processes.

Key Waste-to-Energy Strategies:

- **Anaerobic digestion**: Organic waste is broken down by microorganisms to produce biogas, which can be used for cooking, electricity, and transportation.
- **Incineration with energy recovery**: While incineration is often criticized for air pollution, modern waste-to-energy plants use advanced filtration to generate clean electricity.
- **Gasification and pyrolysis**: High-temperature processes convert waste into syngas and bio-oil, which can be used as an alternative fuel.
- **Algae-based biofuel production**: Industrial carbon waste and wastewater can be used to cultivate algae, which can then be processed into biofuels.

By integrating waste-to-energy solutions, non-recyclable waste can contribute to sustainable energy systems, reducing reliance on fossil fuels and lowering greenhouse gas emissions.

Innovations in Circular Waste Management for Sustainable Restoration

As the world faces increasing environmental challenges, innovative circular waste management solutions are emerging to address pollution, resource depletion, and ecosystem degradation. Traditional waste management systems, which rely on landfilling, incineration, and open dumping, have contributed to air, soil, and water pollution, harming biodiversity and human health.

A circular approach to waste management seeks to transform waste into a resource, keeping materials in productive use for as long as possible while minimizing environmental impact. Advancements in technology, policy, and community-led initiatives are creating new opportunities for waste recovery, recycling, and sustainable ecosystem restoration.

This section explores key innovations in circular waste management, including smart waste tracking, advanced recycling technologies, decentralized waste systems, and circular business models that promote sustainable restoration.

Smart Waste Tracking and Digital Innovations

Technology is playing a crucial role in improving waste management efficiency and resource recovery. Digital tools help monitor waste flows, optimize collection processes, and support data-driven decision-making to reduce waste at the source.

Key Innovations in Smart Waste Tracking:

- **IoT-enabled waste bins**: Smart bins equipped with sensors and real-time data tracking optimize collection schedules, reducing unnecessary transport emissions and landfill overflow.
- **Blockchain for waste traceability**: Blockchain technology creates transparent, tamper-proof records of waste production, disposal, and recycling, ensuring accountability in supply chains.
- **AI-driven sorting systems**: Advanced machine learning algorithms in recycling facilities improve waste separation, increasing the efficiency of plastic, metal, and paper recycling.
- **Mobile apps for waste reduction**: Apps that connect businesses and individuals to waste exchange platforms, where unwanted materials can be repurposed instead of discarded.

By leveraging digital solutions, waste management can become more efficient, data-driven, and aligned with circular economy principles, reducing environmental impact and improving resource recovery.

Advanced Recycling Technologies for Material Recovery

Traditional recycling processes often have limitations due to contamination, mixed materials, and inefficient sorting methods. New recycling technologies are overcoming these barriers by enhancing material recovery and creating higher-quality recycled products.

Cutting-Edge Recycling Innovations:

- **Chemical recycling for plastics**: Unlike conventional mechanical recycling, chemical recycling breaks plastic down into its molecular components, allowing for infinite recyclability without degrading quality.
- **Bio-recycling using enzymes**: Enzyme-based recycling methods break down complex waste materials, such as bioplastics and synthetic textiles, into reusable raw materials.
- **Recycling construction and demolition waste**: Technologies that crush and reprocess concrete, bricks, and metals from old buildings enable the creation of new infrastructure materials.
- **Textile fiber regeneration**: Advanced methods allow cotton, polyester, and synthetic fibers to be separated and re-spun into new clothing, reducing textile waste in landfills.

By adopting innovative recycling techniques, industries can minimize waste production while reintegrating materials into the economy, reducing the need for virgin resource extraction.

Decentralized and Community-Led Waste Solutions

Many traditional waste management systems are centralized, requiring large-scale collection, processing, and disposal operations. However, decentralized approaches empower local communities, businesses, and municipalities to manage waste efficiently while contributing to ecosystem restoration.

Examples of Decentralized Circular Waste Management:

- **Urban composting programs**: Cities establish local composting hubs where organic waste is transformed into fertilizer for urban farms and green spaces.
- **Micro-recycling factories**: Small, community-operated recycling plants process plastic, metal, and glass waste locally, reducing transportation emissions.
- **Waste-to-bioenergy microgrids**: Decentralized systems use food and agricultural waste to generate biogas for local households and businesses.
- **Deposit-refund and incentive programs**: Bottle return schemes, waste buyback centers, and community recycling rewards encourage higher participation in circular waste systems.

By promoting localized waste solutions, communities become more self-sufficient in waste management, supporting economic development and environmental restoration.

Circular Business Models Driving Sustainable Waste Management

The shift toward circular waste management is not only driven by technology but also by business innovation and new economic models. Companies are designing zero-waste supply chains and integrating circular practices into their operations to minimize waste production.

Circular Business Strategies in Waste Management:

- **Product-as-a-service models**: Instead of selling products, companies lease them and take them back for refurbishment and reuse (e.g., leasing electronics, furniture, and industrial equipment).
- **Reusable packaging and container systems**: Businesses eliminate single-use packaging by introducing refillable containers, returnable glass bottles, and biodegradable packaging alternatives.

- **Upcycling and repurposing industries**: Creative industries use discarded materials to make new consumer goods, such as fashion, furniture, and home decor from waste textiles and plastics.
- **Circular procurement policies**: Businesses and governments commit to purchasing products made from recycled materials, creating a strong market for circular economy goods.

By adopting circular business strategies, industries not only reduce waste production but also create sustainable economic opportunities while protecting ecosystems.

Chapter 4: Circular Water Management for Ecosystem Health

Water is a finite and essential resource, supporting both natural ecosystems and human societies. However, unsustainable water use, pollution, and climate change have placed increasing pressure on freshwater supplies, wetlands, and marine environments. Conventional water management systems often follow a linear approach, where water is extracted, used, and discharged as waste, leading to scarcity, contamination, and ecosystem degradation.

A circular water management approach seeks to close the loop by reducing water waste, enhancing efficiency, and promoting reuse and natural filtration systems. By integrating nature-based solutions, advanced recycling technologies, and sustainable infrastructure, circular water strategies help restore ecosystem health, improve water quality, and ensure long-term water security.

This chapter explores efficient water use and recycling in ecosystem restoration, nature-based solutions for water conservation, circular water strategies for urban and rural resilience, and approaches to addressing water pollution through circular interventions. By shifting to circular water systems, societies can protect ecosystems, enhance climate resilience, and secure water for future generations.

Efficient Water Use and Recycling in Ecosystem Restoration

Water is a critical resource for ecosystems, agriculture, industry, and human consumption, yet increasing demand and environmental pressures have led to water scarcity, pollution, and ecosystem degradation. Traditional water management follows a linear approach, where water is extracted, used, and then discharged as wastewater. This system not only depletes freshwater resources but also contributes to water contamination and habitat loss.

A circular water management approach focuses on efficient water use and recycling, ensuring that water remains in circulation for as long as possible while minimizing waste. By integrating sustainable water-use strategies, advanced water recycling technologies, and nature-based solutions, circular water management supports ecosystem restoration, climate resilience, and long-term water security.

This section explores key circular strategies for reducing water waste, enhancing water recycling in restoration efforts, improving wastewater treatment, and promoting decentralized water management systems.

Reducing Water Waste Through Efficiency Measures

One of the most effective ways to protect ecosystems and ensure water sustainability is to reduce unnecessary water consumption. Many industries, agricultural systems, and urban centers use far more water than necessary due to inefficient practices and outdated infrastructure.

Circular Strategies for Water Efficiency:

- **Smart irrigation systems**: Using sensor-based irrigation and drip irrigation to optimize water use in agriculture and landscaping, reducing runoff and evaporation.
- **Leak detection and repair**: Implementing real-time monitoring systems in cities and industries to detect and fix leaks, preventing water loss.
- **Water-efficient appliances and industrial processes**: Encouraging the use of low-flow fixtures, water-efficient cooling systems, and closed-loop industrial processes to reduce water consumption.
- **Behavioral and policy-driven water conservation**: Educating communities on water-saving practices and implementing regulations that limit excessive water use in drought-prone areas.

By prioritizing efficient water use, ecosystems can retain more water for natural processes, agriculture can thrive with less irrigation, and urban areas can reduce their overall water footprint.

Water Recycling and Reuse in Ecosystem Restoration

Recycling water reduces the demand for freshwater extraction while providing a sustainable water source for ecosystem restoration projects. Circular water systems ensure that treated wastewater, stormwater, and industrial effluent can be safely reused for multiple purposes.

Key Water Recycling Strategies for Restoration:

- **Stormwater capture and reuse**: Collecting and treating stormwater for irrigation, groundwater recharge, and wetland restoration.
- **Greywater recycling**: Diverting lightly used household and commercial wastewater (e.g., from sinks and showers) for landscape irrigation and non-potable applications.
- **Treated wastewater for ecosystem rehabilitation**: Using highly treated wastewater to replenish dry riverbeds, wetlands, and degraded lakes, restoring biodiversity and water balance.
- **Desalination with brine management**: Innovative desalination technologies reduce environmental impact by minimizing brine waste and reusing extracted minerals.

Recycled water helps sustain wetlands, forests, and agricultural lands, ensuring that natural ecosystems receive the water they need without further depleting groundwater and river systems.

Improving Wastewater Treatment for Sustainable Water Reuse

Untreated or poorly treated wastewater contributes to water pollution, habitat destruction, and public health risks. Circular wastewater treatment technologies help clean water while recovering valuable nutrients and energy from waste streams.

Innovations in Circular Wastewater Treatment:

- **Biological wastewater treatment**: Utilizing microorganisms and plant-based systems (e.g., constructed wetlands) to naturally purify wastewater.
- **Energy recovery from wastewater**: Converting organic waste in sewage into biogas for renewable energy while improving treatment efficiency.
- **Nutrient recovery and reuse**: Extracting phosphorus and nitrogen from wastewater for use in fertilizers, reducing reliance on synthetic agricultural inputs.
- **Decentralized wastewater treatment**: Small-scale, on-site treatment plants reduce the need for large infrastructure, allowing rural and remote communities to manage water sustainably.

By treating and repurposing wastewater, circular water management reduces pollution, conserves freshwater, and supports ecosystem restoration efforts.

Decentralized and Community-Based Water Management

Many water management systems rely on large-scale infrastructure, which can be expensive and inflexible. Decentralized water systems empower local communities, businesses, and municipalities to manage water resources more efficiently.

Community-Driven Circular Water Strategies:

- **Local rainwater harvesting projects**: Encouraging households and businesses to capture and store rainwater for reuse.

- **Community-led watershed restoration**: Engaging local groups in reforesting watersheds, maintaining wetlands, and protecting river ecosystems.
- **Small-scale water recycling plants**: Enabling communities to treat and reuse their wastewater for agriculture, public sanitation, and landscape irrigation.
- **Policy incentives for water efficiency**: Providing financial incentives for businesses and households that invest in water-saving and recycling technologies.

By empowering local communities, decentralized water management increases resilience to climate change, supports ecosystem restoration, and reduces reliance on large-scale water supply networks.

Nature-Based Solutions for Water Conservation

Water is a fundamental resource for both ecosystems and human societies, yet unsustainable management has led to scarcity, pollution, and ecosystem degradation. Conventional water conservation strategies often rely on engineered solutions, such as dams and pipelines, which can disrupt natural water cycles and further stress ecosystems. In contrast, NbS leverage natural processes to enhance water conservation, restore hydrological balance, and improve climate resilience.

Nature-based solutions focus on working with ecosystems rather than against them, using forests, wetlands, soils, and vegetation to regulate water flows, reduce evaporation, and improve water retention. These approaches contribute to long-term water security while enhancing biodiversity, carbon sequestration, and community resilience.

This section explores key nature-based solutions for water conservation, including wetland restoration, reforestation, soil management, and urban water-sensitive design.

Wetland Restoration for Water Storage and Filtration

Wetlands are natural water reservoirs that store excess rainfall, filter pollutants, and support diverse ecosystems. However, widespread wetland degradation due to urban expansion, agriculture, and infrastructure development has reduced their ability to regulate water cycles.

How Wetlands Contribute to Water Conservation:

- **Natural flood control**: Wetlands absorb excess rainfall, reducing the risk of flooding and soil erosion.
- **Water filtration**: Wetland plants and soils trap sediments, nutrients, and pollutants, improving water quality before it enters rivers and lakes.
- **Groundwater recharge**: Wetlands slow water movement, allowing infiltration into underground aquifers, replenishing groundwater supplies.
- **Biodiversity support**: Restored wetlands provide habitats for birds, fish, and aquatic species, enhancing ecological balance.

By protecting and restoring wetlands, communities can secure freshwater resources, prevent pollution, and build resilience against droughts and floods.

Reforestation and Agroforestry for Water Retention

Forests play a crucial role in water conservation and climate regulation, influencing rainfall patterns and maintaining water availability. However, deforestation reduces water retention capacity, leading to drying rivers, soil erosion, and declining groundwater levels.

Key Water Conservation Benefits of Forests:

- **Enhanced rainfall absorption**: Tree roots increase soil permeability, improving water infiltration and reducing surface runoff.
- **Soil moisture retention**: Leaf litter and organic matter enhance soil structure, reducing evaporation and supporting crop growth.
- **Reduced erosion and sedimentation**: Forests stabilize soils, preventing sediments from clogging rivers and reservoirs.
- **Improved microclimates**: Forest cover regulates temperature and humidity, supporting sustainable agriculture and water availability.

Agroforestry as a Circular Water Strategy:

Agroforestry integrates trees and crops, improving soil fertility, water retention, and resilience to droughts. Techniques include:

- **Windbreaks and shelterbelts**: Rows of trees reduce water loss from evaporation in dry regions.
- **Alley cropping**: Planting crops between trees helps reduce runoff and improve soil moisture balance.
- **Shade-grown agriculture**: Coffee and cocoa plantations benefit from reduced water stress under tree cover.

Reforestation and agroforestry restore degraded landscapes, ensuring long-term water sustainability while supporting climate adaptation.

Soil and Watershed Management for Water Efficiency

Healthy soils are essential for water conservation, acting as sponges that absorb, store, and slowly release water. However, intensive farming, deforestation, and urbanization have led to soil degradation, reducing water-holding capacity.

Circular Soil and Watershed Management Strategies:

- **Cover cropping**: Planting cover crops prevents soil drying and increases water infiltration.
- **Terracing and contour farming**: These techniques slow water flow on slopes, reducing runoff and preventing erosion.
- **Biochar soil amendments**: Adding biochar to soil enhances water retention and nutrient availability, improving agricultural sustainability.
- **Watershed restoration**: Protecting riverbanks and planting vegetation along watersheds reduces sedimentation and pollution, preserving freshwater ecosystems.

By integrating soil and watershed management, agricultural and rural communities can retain more water, reduce irrigation needs, and build resilience to droughts.

Water-Sensitive Urban Design for Sustainable Cities

Urban areas experience high water demand, stormwater runoff, and pollution, making water conservation a critical priority. WSUD integrates natural systems into cities, reducing water waste while enhancing green infrastructure.

Key WSUD Strategies for Water Conservation:

- **Permeable pavements**: Instead of traditional asphalt, permeable surfaces allow rainwater to infiltrate the ground, replenishing groundwater.
- **Green roofs and rain gardens**: Vegetation on rooftops and in urban spaces captures rainwater, reducing stormwater runoff and urban flooding.
- **Rainwater harvesting systems**: Collecting and storing rainwater for non-potable uses like irrigation and cooling reduces demand on municipal supplies.
- **Decentralized greywater recycling**: Treating and reusing household and commercial wastewater for landscaping and toilet flushing conserves potable water.

By integrating nature into urban planning, WSUD enhances water efficiency, reduces environmental impact, and promotes climate resilience.

Circular Water Strategies for Urban and Rural Resilience

Water security is a critical issue in both urban and rural areas, where population growth, climate change, and inefficient water use are straining available resources. Traditional water management follows a linear model, where water is extracted, used, and discharged, leading to waste, pollution, and increased pressure on freshwater supplies. This approach is unsustainable, particularly in regions facing water scarcity, extreme weather events, and ecosystem degradation.

A circular water management approach ensures that water resources are used efficiently, reused safely, and reintegrated into the environment in a way that enhances resilience. By closing the water loop, cities and rural areas can reduce dependence on new water sources, improve environmental sustainability, and build resilient systems that adapt to climate variability.

This section explores key circular water strategies that strengthen resilience in urban and rural settings, including integrated water resource management, decentralized water systems, nature-based solutions, and water reuse initiatives.

Integrated Water Resource Management for Holistic Water Use

A circular approach to water management requires considering the entire water cycle rather than managing water in isolated sectors. Integrated Water Resource Management (IWRM) promotes a coordinated and sustainable use of water across agriculture, industry, and households to prevent over-extraction and pollution.

Key IWRM Strategies for Resilience:

- **Balancing urban and rural water use**: Ensuring that agriculture, industry, and residential areas share water resources equitably.
- **Protecting upstream watersheds**: Managing forests, wetlands, and rivers to maintain natural water flows and prevent pollution.
- **Implementing demand-based water allocation**: Using smart meters and real-time monitoring to reduce overuse and water loss in cities and rural communities.
- **Multi-sector collaboration**: Encouraging governments, industries, and local communities to develop sustainable water-sharing agreements.

By managing water as a shared resource, cities and rural areas can become more climate-resilient and efficient in their water use.

Decentralized Water Systems for Localized Water Resilience

Large-scale, centralized water infrastructure is costly, complex, and vulnerable to climate-related disruptions, such as droughts and floods. Decentralized water systems empower local communities, households, and businesses to manage water more efficiently at a smaller scale, reducing dependence on centralized supply networks.

Circular Decentralized Water Strategies:

- **Rainwater harvesting systems**: Collecting and storing rainwater for household, agricultural, and industrial use reduces demand on municipal supplies.
- **Localized water treatment plants**: Small-scale water purification units enable remote or underserved communities to access clean drinking water without relying on large pipelines.

- **Community-led water governance**: Encouraging local cooperatives and water user groups to manage and distribute water resources fairly and sustainably.
- **Decentralized wastewater treatment**: Treating greywater and sewage at the community or household level reduces pressure on overburdened urban water systems.

By shifting to decentralized solutions, cities and rural communities can increase water access, reduce infrastructure costs, and improve resilience to climate disruptions.

Nature-Based Water Solutions for Climate Adaptation

In both urban and rural areas, NbS enhance resilience by restoring natural water processes and protecting ecosystems from extreme weather events. These solutions work in harmony with natural landscapes to regulate water flows, reduce floods, and improve water storage.

Nature-Based Solutions for Water Resilience:

- **Restoring wetlands and floodplains**: These natural buffers store excess rainwater, preventing flooding in cities and protecting farmland from drought.
- **Green infrastructure in cities**: Permeable pavements, green roofs, and bioswales reduce stormwater runoff and increase groundwater recharge.
- **Reforestation and agroforestry**: Trees improve water retention in soils, reducing drought impacts in rural areas.
- **Regenerative agricultural water management**: Techniques like mulching, contour farming, and cover cropping help conserve water in farming communities.

By integrating nature-based solutions, urban and rural areas can enhance climate adaptation, prevent water shortages, and improve ecosystem resilience.

Water Reuse and Recycling for Sustainable Supply

Rather than discarding wastewater, circular water strategies emphasize recycling and safe reuse to extend the lifecycle of water resources. Water reuse is essential for maintaining a stable supply in regions facing droughts, population growth, and increasing water demands.

Circular Approaches to Water Reuse:

- **Greywater recycling**: Lightly used household water from showers, sinks, and laundry can be filtered and reused for irrigation and flushing toilets.
- **Treated wastewater for irrigation**: Municipal wastewater treatment plants can supply cleaned water for agriculture, reducing pressure on freshwater sources.
- **Industrial water recycling**: Factories can implement closed-loop water systems to reduce the need for continuous freshwater extraction.
- **Desalination with brine recovery**: In coastal cities, desalination can provide freshwater while minimizing waste disposal impacts through brine concentration and reuse.

By adopting water recycling systems, cities and rural communities reduce dependency on freshwater sources while maintaining a secure and sustainable supply.

Addressing Water Pollution Through Circular Interventions

Water pollution is a major global challenge, affecting ecosystems, human health, and economic activities. Industrial discharge, agricultural runoff, plastic waste, and untreated sewage have severely contaminated rivers, lakes, and oceans, leading to biodiversity loss, water scarcity, and environmental degradation. Traditional approaches to managing water pollution focus primarily on treatment and removal, but these solutions often fail to address the root causes of contamination.

A circular approach to water pollution prioritizes preventing contamination at the source, recovering valuable resources from wastewater, and reintegrating treated water back into the ecosystem or economy. By shifting from linear water use to closed-loop systems, industries, municipalities, and communities can reduce pollution while ensuring that water remains clean, available, and sustainable.

This section explores key circular interventions to tackle water pollution, including wastewater recovery, nature-based water treatment, industrial water reuse, and plastic waste reduction.

Wastewater Recovery and Resource Extraction

Instead of treating wastewater as a waste product, circular interventions view it as a valuable resource that can be recovered and reused. Modern wastewater treatment processes allow for the extraction of nutrients, energy, and clean water, reducing pollution while creating useful byproducts.

Circular Strategies for Wastewater Recovery:

- **Nutrient recovery for agriculture**: Extracting phosphorus and nitrogen from wastewater to produce fertilizers, reducing reliance on synthetic inputs and preventing water pollution from excess nutrients.
- **Water reuse in industrial processes**: Treated wastewater can be recycled within factories for cooling, cleaning, and manufacturing, reducing water extraction from freshwater sources.
- **Energy generation from organic waste**: Anaerobic digestion of sewage sludge and food waste produces biogas, which can be used for electricity or heating.

- **Decentralized wastewater treatment**: On-site and community-based wastewater systems reduce pollution by treating and reusing water locally before it enters larger waterways.

By closing the wastewater loop, cities and industries can reduce water contamination, recover valuable resources, and create a more sustainable water cycle.

Nature-Based Water Treatment Solutions

NbS use natural processes to filter pollutants, restore water quality, and reduce dependence on energy-intensive treatment plants. These approaches integrate vegetation, soils, and microbial activity to purify water while enhancing biodiversity and ecosystem resilience.

Key Nature-Based Water Treatment Techniques:

- **Constructed wetlands**: Artificial wetland systems filter out heavy metals, excess nutrients, and organic pollutants from wastewater before it is released into rivers and lakes.
- **Riparian buffer zones**: Planting trees and vegetation along riverbanks helps trap sediments and agricultural runoff, preventing pollutants from entering water bodies.
- **Floating treatment wetlands**: Aquatic plants grown on floating platforms absorb pollutants from contaminated lakes, ponds, and reservoirs.
- **Green infrastructure in cities**: Bioswales, rain gardens, and permeable pavements reduce urban water pollution by capturing and filtering stormwater runoff before it reaches drainage systems.

These nature-based interventions improve water quality, restore degraded ecosystems, and provide long-term climate resilience while reducing pollution.

Industrial Water Reuse and Zero-Discharge Systems

Industries are a major source of water pollution, releasing toxic chemicals, heavy metals, and untreated waste into water bodies. A circular industrial water management system ensures that wastewater is treated, purified, and reused within production cycles, minimizing both pollution and water consumption.

Circular Solutions for Industrial Water Management:

- **Closed-loop water recycling**: Factories implement water reuse systems that allow them to continuously treat and recirculate water, reducing pollution.
- **Zero-liquid discharge (ZLD) systems**: Advanced treatment technologies remove all liquid waste from industrial effluent, recovering clean water and valuable byproducts such as salts and minerals.
- **Green chemistry and pollution-free production**: Redesigning manufacturing processes to eliminate hazardous chemicals, ensuring that discharged water is non-toxic.
- **Reverse osmosis and membrane filtration**: High-tech purification systems remove contaminants, enabling safe water reuse within industries and municipalities.

By adopting circular industrial water management, businesses can reduce their environmental impact, improve operational efficiency, and protect freshwater ecosystems.

Reducing Plastic Waste to Prevent Water Contamination

Plastic pollution is one of the most severe water contamination issues, with millions of tons of plastic entering rivers and oceans annually. Circular waste interventions aim to prevent plastic waste at its source, ensuring that materials remain in use rather than polluting waterways.

Circular Strategies to Address Plastic Water Pollution:

- **Expanding deposit-return schemes**: Encouraging consumers to return plastic bottles and containers for reuse and recycling, reducing litter in water bodies.
- **Biodegradable and compostable alternatives**: Replacing petroleum-based plastics with bio-based materials that decompose naturally.
- **Waste interception and cleanup technologies**: Using river booms, trash traps, and ocean-cleaning robots to remove floating plastic waste before it reaches the open sea.
- **Microplastic filtration in wastewater treatment**: Advanced filters prevent tiny plastic particles from entering lakes, rivers, and oceans.

By designing out plastic waste and improving recycling systems, circular strategies protect marine life, improve water quality, and reduce pollution at its source.

Chapter 5: Circular Agriculture and Land Restoration

Agriculture is essential for global food security, but conventional farming practices have contributed to soil degradation, water scarcity, deforestation, and biodiversity loss. The reliance on intensive monoculture, chemical fertilizers, and excessive irrigation has led to declining soil fertility and ecosystem instability. Additionally, agricultural waste and emissions have further strained natural resources.

A circular approach to agriculture and land restoration seeks to close resource loops, enhance soil health, and minimize waste, ensuring that food production remains sustainable while regenerating degraded ecosystems. By integrating regenerative farming, agroecology, waste repurposing, and soil conservation techniques, circular agriculture promotes long-term environmental and economic resilience.

This chapter explores sustainable agricultural models for degraded land, agroecology and soil regeneration, circular nutrient management, and sustainable land-use strategies. By transitioning to circular agricultural systems, societies can restore ecosystems, improve food security, and reduce agriculture's environmental footprint while ensuring productive landscapes for future generations.

Sustainable Agricultural Models for Degraded Land

Agricultural expansion and intensive farming have led to widespread land degradation, resulting in soil erosion, nutrient depletion, loss of biodiversity, and declining water retention capacity. These challenges threaten food security, climate resilience, and rural livelihoods, particularly in regions where overcultivation and deforestation have left landscapes barren. Traditional agricultural practices often rely on high-input chemical fertilizers, monocropping, and excessive irrigation, which further degrade land over time.

A circular approach to agriculture focuses on restoring soil health, reducing resource waste, and integrating regenerative farming practices that ensure long-term productivity while enhancing environmental resilience. By adopting sustainable agricultural models, farmers can rehabilitate degraded land, increase soil fertility, and maintain ecosystem balance without overexploiting natural resources.

This section explores key sustainable agricultural models that contribute to land restoration, including regenerative farming, agroecology, conservation agriculture, and integrated land management systems.

Regenerative Farming for Soil Restoration

Regenerative farming prioritizes soil health by enhancing organic matter, improving biodiversity, and restoring degraded ecosystems. Unlike conventional methods that deplete soil fertility, regenerative farming works with natural processes to rebuild soil structure and nutrient levels.

Core Principles of Regenerative Farming:

- **Minimal soil disturbance (no-till farming)**: Reduces soil erosion, retains moisture, and supports soil microbes essential for nutrient cycling.
- **Cover cropping**: Planting cover crops such as legumes and clover prevents soil depletion, reduces weeds, and enhances organic matter.
- **Compost and organic fertilizers**: Using compost, manure, and biochar restores nutrients and promotes microbial activity in degraded soils.

- **Holistic grazing management**: Rotational grazing prevents overgrazing, allowing pastures to regenerate and improve soil carbon sequestration.

By restoring soil ecosystems, regenerative farming increases water retention, prevents erosion, and enhances long-term agricultural sustainability.

Agroecology for Biodiversity and Resilience

Agroecology integrates traditional ecological knowledge with modern farming techniques, focusing on biodiversity, soil regeneration, and resource efficiency. This model is particularly effective in revitalizing degraded landscapes by creating self-sustaining agricultural systems.

Agroecological Practices for Land Restoration:

- **Polyculture farming**: Growing multiple crop species together enhances nutrient cycling, reduces pest outbreaks, and increases overall resilience.
- **Agroforestry integration**: Combining trees, shrubs, and crops improves soil fertility, prevents erosion, and provides additional income sources for farmers.
- **Natural pest management**: Encouraging beneficial insects and using botanical pesticides reduces reliance on chemical pesticides that harm soil health.
- **Soil moisture conservation**: Terracing and mulching techniques prevent water runoff, ensuring soil remains hydrated during dry seasons.

Agroecology strengthens ecosystem resilience, enabling degraded lands to recover naturally while maintaining food production capacity.

Conservation Agriculture for Land Rehabilitation

Conservation agriculture is a farming system designed to preserve soil integrity and ecosystem balance by using low-impact cultivation techniques. It focuses on sustaining agricultural productivity while minimizing environmental degradation.

Key Conservation Agriculture Techniques:

- **Reduced tillage and soil conservation structures**: Prevents soil compaction, enhances root penetration, and reduces carbon loss.
- **Crop rotation and intercropping**: Improves soil health, reduces pests, and diversifies farmers' incomes by integrating legumes, grains, and vegetables.
- **Integrated nutrient management**: Balances organic and mineral fertilizers to restore soil fertility without over-reliance on synthetic inputs.
- **Rainwater harvesting for irrigation**: Capturing and storing rainwater reduces dependence on external water sources, supporting dryland farming.

By implementing conservation agriculture, farmers can restore degraded land while maintaining high-yield, low-impact agricultural production.

Integrated Land Management for Sustainable Landscapes

Integrated land management systems take a holistic approach by combining agriculture, forestry, and water management to rehabilitate degraded landscapes. This model ensures that all elements of the landscape—soil, water, vegetation, and biodiversity—are managed in a coordinated way.

Components of Integrated Land Management:

- **Agro-silvopastoral systems**: Integrates trees, crops, and livestock, balancing food production with ecosystem restoration.

- **Soil and water conservation measures**: Constructing check dams, retention ponds, and bio-swales enhances groundwater recharge and reduces soil erosion.
- **Sustainable land-use zoning**: Dividing landscapes into areas for farming, forestry, and conservation to optimize ecosystem functions.
- **Community-led land restoration**: Engaging local communities in afforestation, watershed protection, and regenerative agriculture projects.

By using integrated land management, degraded land can be rehabilitated into productive and ecologically stable landscapes, ensuring long-term resilience for both people and nature.

Agroecology and Soil Regeneration

Soil is the foundation of agriculture, supporting plant growth, biodiversity, and water retention. However, modern agricultural practices, such as monocropping, excessive tillage, and chemical-intensive farming, have degraded soils, leading to loss of fertility, erosion, and declining productivity. As soil health deteriorates, it becomes increasingly difficult to sustain food production while maintaining environmental balance.

Agroecology offers a holistic approach to farming that prioritizes soil regeneration, biodiversity, and ecological balance. By integrating traditional knowledge with modern sustainable practices, agroecology restores soil fertility, reduces reliance on synthetic inputs, and promotes resilient food systems.

This section explores key agroecological strategies for soil regeneration, including soil-building techniques, crop diversity, natural fertilizers, and ecosystem-based farming methods that enhance soil health while ensuring long-term agricultural productivity.

Building Healthy Soils Through Organic Matter Enrichment

One of the core principles of agroecology is restoring and maintaining soil organic matter, which improves nutrient availability, moisture retention, and microbial activity. Organic matter acts as a natural fertilizer, supporting soil structure and enhancing its ability to retain carbon and nutrients.

Agroecological Methods for Soil Organic Matter Improvement:

- **Composting**: Organic waste, such as crop residues, food scraps, and manure, is composted to create nutrient-rich soil amendments that improve fertility and microbial diversity.
- **Biochar application**: Biochar, produced from biomass waste, enhances soil structure, water retention, and carbon sequestration while preventing nutrient leaching.
- **Mulching**: Covering soil with straw, leaves, or plant residues reduces water loss, protects against erosion, and promotes soil biodiversity.
- **Green manure cover crops**: Leguminous cover crops, such as clover and alfalfa, fix nitrogen in the soil while preventing erosion and enhancing organic matter content.

By increasing organic matter levels, soils become more fertile, resilient, and productive without the need for excessive synthetic fertilizers.

Crop Diversity and Agroforestry for Soil Resilience

Diverse cropping systems enhance soil health and resilience by mimicking natural ecosystems, improving nutrient cycling, and preventing soil depletion. Unlike monoculture, which exhausts specific nutrients, crop diversity strengthens soil fertility by balancing nutrient demand.

Agroecological Strategies for Enhancing Soil Resilience:

- **Polyculture farming**: Growing multiple crop species together increases nutrient diversity in the soil, reducing pest and disease pressure.
- **Crop rotation**: Alternating different crops each season prevents soil degradation by varying nutrient uptake and replenishment cycles.
- **Agroforestry systems**: Integrating trees with crops and livestock enhances shade, wind protection, and organic matter input, supporting long-term soil regeneration.
- **Perennial farming**: Cultivating perennial plants and grasses stabilizes soil, prevents erosion, and reduces reliance on seasonal replanting.

By promoting crop diversity and agroforestry, soils become more resilient to climate variability and long-term degradation.

Using Natural Fertilizers and Biological Soil Enhancements

Synthetic fertilizers provide short-term nutrient boosts but often degrade soil health over time by disrupting microbial communities and causing chemical imbalances. Agroecology promotes the use of natural and biological fertilizers, which improve soil structure and nutrient availability without harming the environment.

Sustainable Soil Fertility Management Approaches:

- **Vermicomposting**: Earthworm composting produces nutrient-rich vermicast, which enhances soil fertility and microbial activity.
- **Liquid biofertilizers**: Fermented plant extracts and beneficial microbial solutions increase nutrient absorption and soil resilience.
- **Mycorrhizal fungi inoculation**: Beneficial fungi form symbiotic relationships with plant roots, enhancing nutrient uptake and improving soil structure.

- **Natural pest and disease control**: Using botanical pesticides, neem oil, and beneficial insect habitats reduces the need for chemical inputs that degrade soil biodiversity.

By prioritizing natural fertilizers, agroecology supports long-term soil health and self-sustaining nutrient cycles.

Ecosystem-Based Farming for Sustainable Soil Management

Agroecology extends beyond soil treatment by integrating farming with natural ecosystem processes. This ensures that soil regeneration happens naturally, reducing dependence on external inputs while improving farm productivity.

Ecosystem-Based Soil Management Strategies:

- **Integrated pest management (IPM)**: Encouraging natural predators and plant-based pest deterrents reduces chemical pesticide use, preserving soil biodiversity.
- **Regenerative grazing**: Rotational grazing prevents overgrazing, allowing soil to recover and rebuild organic matter levels.
- **Water conservation techniques**: Techniques such as swales, rainwater harvesting, and keyline design help retain moisture in soil, preventing desertification.
- **Restoring degraded lands with native vegetation**: Planting native species improves soil structure, carbon sequestration, and water infiltration.

By aligning farming with natural processes, ecosystem-based approaches enhance soil regeneration, biodiversity, and climate resilience.

Closing Nutrient Loops: Organic Waste as a Soil Resource

Agricultural productivity and soil health depend on nutrient availability, yet conventional farming practices have created linear nutrient cycles where nutrients are extracted from the soil, used for crop growth, and often lost as waste. This one-way flow depletes soil fertility, increases reliance on synthetic fertilizers, and contributes to environmental issues such as water pollution, greenhouse gas emissions, and soil degradation.

A circular approach to nutrient management focuses on recycling organic waste back into the soil, creating closed-loop systems that regenerate fertility naturally. By transforming crop residues, food waste, livestock manure, and other organic materials into valuable soil resources, nutrient loops can be closed to support long-term agricultural sustainability.

This section explores how organic waste can be effectively reintegrated into farming systems, including composting, biofertilizers, livestock waste recycling, and innovative nutrient recovery technologies.

Composting: Transforming Organic Waste into Soil Fertility

Composting is one of the most effective ways to recycle nutrients from organic waste back into the soil. By allowing microorganisms to break down plant and food waste, composting produces a nutrient-rich soil amendment that enhances soil structure and fertility.

Key Benefits of Composting for Soil Health:

- **Improves soil structure**: Enhances aeration and water retention, reducing the risk of erosion and drought stress.
- **Replenishes essential nutrients**: Restores nitrogen, phosphorus, and potassium without the need for synthetic fertilizers.

- **Supports beneficial soil microbes**: Increases microbial diversity, which helps break down organic matter and cycle nutrients efficiently.
- **Reduces landfill waste and greenhouse gas emissions**: Diverting organic waste from landfills prevents methane emissions and promotes sustainable waste management.

Types of Composting Systems:

- **Traditional aerobic composting**: Organic materials decompose through oxygen exposure, producing stable, nutrient-rich compost.
- **Vermicomposting**: Earthworms process organic waste, creating highly fertile vermicast, which boosts plant growth.
- **Bokashi fermentation**: An anaerobic composting method that rapidly converts food waste into usable organic matter.

By integrating composting into agricultural practices, farmers can reduce reliance on chemical fertilizers and restore soil nutrients naturally.

Biofertilizers and Microbial Soil Enhancements

Biofertilizers use living microorganisms to enhance nutrient availability in the soil, reducing the need for synthetic inputs while improving long-term soil fertility. These natural fertilizers promote biological nitrogen fixation, phosphorus solubilization, and organic matter decomposition, contributing to a self-sustaining nutrient cycle.

Types of Biofertilizers and Their Benefits:

- **Nitrogen-fixing bacteria (e.g., Rhizobium, Azotobacter)**: Converts atmospheric nitrogen into a form that plants can absorb, reducing the need for nitrogen fertilizers.

- **Phosphate-solubilizing bacteria (e.g., Pseudomonas, Bacillus)**: Releases bound phosphorus in the soil, making it available for plant uptake.
- **Mycorrhizal fungi**: Forms symbiotic relationships with plant roots, enhancing nutrient and water absorption while stabilizing soil structure.
- **Liquid biofertilizers**: Microbial solutions applied to soils or crops to stimulate root development and improve soil health.

Biofertilizers create a natural, renewable way to maintain soil fertility, reducing environmental impacts associated with synthetic fertilizers.

Recycling Livestock Manure for Soil Nutrient Enrichment

Animal waste is a valuable organic resource that can be effectively recycled back into farming systems to close nutrient loops. However, improper disposal can lead to water pollution and greenhouse gas emissions. Sustainable manure management ensures that livestock waste is processed safely and reintegrated into the soil without environmental harm.

Sustainable Manure Management Strategies:

- **Manure composting**: Reduces pathogens and odors while producing a stable, nutrient-rich soil amendment.
- **Anaerobic digestion for biogas and fertilizer**: Converts livestock waste into renewable energy (biogas) and nutrient-rich digestate for soil application.
- **Manure-based biochar**: Pyrolyzing manure produces a carbon-rich soil enhancer, improving water retention and carbon sequestration.
- **Controlled manure spreading**: Applying manure in precise amounts and timing prevents nutrient runoff and maximizes soil benefits.

By integrating livestock waste into sustainable nutrient management, farms can reduce reliance on chemical fertilizers while improving soil health and productivity.

Innovative Nutrient Recovery Technologies

Emerging technologies are improving the efficiency of nutrient recovery from organic waste, creating new opportunities for circular agriculture. These innovations help reclaim valuable nutrients from food waste, wastewater, and agricultural residues, preventing pollution while enhancing soil fertility.

Key Nutrient Recovery Innovations:

- **Struvite precipitation from wastewater**: Extracts phosphorus and magnesium from wastewater to produce a slow-release fertilizer.
- **Hydrothermal carbonization**: Converts food waste and biomass into carbon-rich soil amendments, reducing waste and enhancing soil structure.
- **Black soldier fly composting**: Uses insect larvae to break down organic waste, producing protein-rich animal feed and nutrient-rich compost.
- **Circular aquaponics systems**: Combines fish farming with plant cultivation, where nutrient-rich fish waste fertilizes crops, creating a closed-loop system.

These technologies contribute to sustainable nutrient cycling, reducing agricultural waste while maintaining long-term soil productivity.

Rewilding and Land Reclamation Through Circular Approaches

Decades of deforestation, industrial activities, urban expansion, and intensive agriculture have left vast areas of land degraded, barren, and unsuitable for biodiversity or productive use. Conventional land reclamation methods often rely on engineered interventions that may not fully restore ecosystem functions or create self-sustaining landscapes. However, circular approaches to rewilding and land reclamation focus on working with nature to restore degraded environments while ensuring long-term ecological and economic benefits.

Rewilding and circular land reclamation strategies revitalize landscapes by enhancing biodiversity, restoring natural cycles, and reintegrating waste and organic materials into ecosystems. By mimicking natural processes and promoting sustainable resource use, circular approaches help create resilient, self-sustaining environments that benefit both people and wildlife.

This section explores key circular strategies for land reclamation, including natural succession, regenerative soil building, waste-to-resource applications, and biodiversity-driven ecosystem restoration.

Natural Succession and Passive Rewilding

One of the most effective and low-impact approaches to land reclamation is allowing nature to regenerate through natural succession. Passive rewilding involves limiting human intervention, allowing plants, animals, and microbial life to gradually restore degraded landscapes.

Key Principles of Passive Rewilding:

- **Allowing natural vegetation regrowth**: Abandoned agricultural fields and post-industrial sites recover naturally when native plant species colonize the land.
- **Encouraging wildlife return**: As habitats regenerate, wildlife corridors enable species migration and ecosystem recovery.

- **Restoring hydrological balance**: Allowing wetlands, rivers, and groundwater systems to re-establish their natural flow patterns improves land stability.
- **Removing human pressures**: Reducing livestock overgrazing and limiting deforestation enables ecosystem recovery without intensive human involvement.

By allowing ecosystems to regenerate naturally, passive rewilding provides a cost-effective, low-maintenance approach to restoring degraded landscapes.

Regenerative Soil Building for Land Restoration

Degraded lands often suffer from poor soil quality, erosion, and nutrient depletion, making them unsuitable for reforestation or agriculture. Circular soil restoration techniques improve fertility by returning organic matter, enhancing microbial life, and increasing water retention.

Circular Strategies for Soil Regeneration:

- **Compost and biochar applications**: Enriching degraded soils with organic compost and biochar improves structure, retains moisture, and increases carbon sequestration.
- **Cover cropping and green manure**: Introducing nitrogen-fixing plants like clover and legumes restores essential soil nutrients.
- **Mycorrhizal fungi inoculation**: Encouraging beneficial fungi enhances nutrient absorption and plant resilience in degraded soils.
- **Mulching and erosion control**: Using organic mulch and plant barriers reduces soil erosion, stabilizing land and supporting vegetation growth.

Through regenerative soil management, degraded lands can transition into productive ecosystems that support plant growth, water retention, and biodiversity.

Waste-to-Resource Applications for Land Reclamation

Circular economy principles can accelerate land restoration by repurposing organic and industrial waste to improve soil health, rebuild ecosystems, and reduce environmental pollution. Instead of treating waste as a burden, it can be reintegrated into landscapes as a valuable resource.

Circular Waste Applications for Land Restoration:

- **Recycled construction materials for habitat creation**: Using reclaimed bricks, concrete, and wood to create wildlife shelters, erosion barriers, and artificial reefs.
- **Bioremediation of contaminated lands**: Deploying bacteria and fungi to break down oil spills, chemical pollutants, and heavy metals in degraded soils.
- **Organic waste conversion into soil amendments**: Transforming food waste, crop residues, and livestock manure into nutrient-rich compost for land reclamation.
- **Mine site rehabilitation using treated industrial byproducts**: Using alkaline byproducts from industrial processes to neutralize acidic soils in former mining areas.

By turning waste into a resource, circular land restoration reduces dependency on new materials while accelerating ecological recovery.

Biodiversity-Driven Ecosystem Restoration

Ecosystems are intricately connected, and restoring degraded land requires a biodiversity-first approach that reintroduces key species, native plants, and ecological interactions to rebuild self-sustaining landscapes.

Circular Strategies for Biodiversity Restoration:

- **Native species reintroduction**: Planting native trees, grasses, and shrubs supports pollinators, herbivores, and predators, rebuilding ecosystem balance.
- **Wildlife corridors and habitat connectivity**: Restoring forests, wetlands, and grasslands creates connected landscapes where species can migrate freely.
- **Beaver and wetland restoration projects**: Encouraging beaver populations to naturally engineer water flow, which improves wetland health and soil hydration.
- **Rewilding with keystone species**: Introducing species like wolves, bison, or large herbivores helps control populations and restore ecological balance.

By focusing on biodiversity, land restoration efforts become more effective, resilient, and self-sustaining over time.

Chapter 6: Circular Bioeconomy and Biodiversity Protection

The bioeconomy refers to the sustainable use of biological resources, such as plants, microorganisms, and organic waste, to create food, energy, materials, and chemicals while minimizing environmental impact. However, conventional resource extraction and production systems often deplete biodiversity, degrade ecosystems, and generate significant waste, threatening long-term ecological balance.

A circular bioeconomy integrates regenerative practices, resource efficiency, and waste valorization to ensure that biological materials are continuously cycled within ecosystems rather than discarded. This approach not only reduces pressure on natural resources but also actively contributes to biodiversity protection, habitat restoration, and climate resilience.

This chapter explores key strategies for implementing a circular bioeconomy, including sustainable use of biological resources, innovative bio-based materials, biodiversity-driven industrial solutions, and regenerative land management. By transitioning to circular bioeconomic models, societies can support thriving ecosystems, reduce waste, and create a sustainable future based on renewable biological resources.

Using Biological Resources in a Sustainable Manner

Biological resources, including forests, fisheries, agricultural products, and microorganisms, play a critical role in supporting economies, providing food, and maintaining ecological balance. However, unsustainable extraction, overharvesting, and inefficient use of these resources have led to deforestation, biodiversity loss, soil degradation, and ecosystem instability. The traditional linear model of resource use, which prioritizes short-term economic gains, often depletes biological materials faster than they can regenerate, creating long-term environmental and economic challenges.

A circular approach to biological resource management ensures that materials are used efficiently, waste is minimized, and ecosystems remain healthy. By integrating sustainable harvesting, responsible production, regenerative practices, and biodiversity conservation, industries can continue benefiting from biological resources without compromising future availability.

This section explores key strategies for using biological resources sustainably, including responsible resource extraction, closed-loop agricultural systems, bio-based material innovation, and ecosystem-based resource management.

Responsible Resource Extraction and Regeneration

Many industries rely on biological raw materials, such as timber, fisheries, and plant-based products, but unsustainable extraction can lead to ecosystem collapse and long-term supply chain vulnerabilities. Implementing responsible resource management practices ensures that these resources remain available and renewable over time.

Sustainable Extraction Strategies:

- **Selective harvesting in forestry**: Rather than clear-cutting forests, selective logging allows mature trees to be harvested while younger trees continue growing, maintaining biodiversity.
- **Sustainable fishing practices**: Quotas, seasonal restrictions, and marine protected areas (MPAs) help prevent overfishing and support marine ecosystem recovery.
- **Ethical wild harvesting of plants**: Ensuring that medicinal plants, herbs, and wild foods are gathered at sustainable rates prevents species decline.
- **Community-managed resource programs**: Local stewardship initiatives allow indigenous and rural communities to oversee sustainable use of forests, fisheries, and grasslands.

By adopting responsible extraction methods, biological resources can regenerate naturally, ensuring long-term environmental and economic stability.

Closed-Loop Agricultural Systems for Sustainable Resource Use

Agriculture is a major consumer of land, water, and biological inputs, and conventional practices often lead to soil depletion, nutrient loss, and waste accumulation. A closed-loop agricultural system recycles biological resources efficiently, reducing dependence on external inputs while improving resilience.

Circular Agriculture Strategies:

- **Integrated crop-livestock systems**: Livestock manure is used as a natural fertilizer for crops, reducing the need for synthetic fertilizers.
- **Regenerative soil management**: Crop rotation, cover cropping, and no-till farming enhance soil fertility and reduce land degradation.
- **Aquaponics and permaculture**: Combining fish farming with plant cultivation creates a self-sustaining ecosystem where nutrients are continuously cycled.
- **Organic waste repurposing**: Converting crop residues and food waste into compost or bioenergy minimizes waste and enhances soil productivity.

By integrating circular agriculture techniques, farmers can maximize biological resource efficiency while reducing environmental impact.

Bio-Based Material Innovation for a Sustainable Economy

Replacing fossil fuel-derived materials with renewable, bio-based alternatives is key to reducing environmental impact. A circular bioeconomy promotes sustainable materials that are biodegradable, recyclable, and derived from renewable sources.

Innovative Bio-Based Materials:

- **Bioplastics and bio-composites**: Made from corn starch, algae, and cellulose, these alternatives replace petroleum-based plastics while reducing pollution.
- **Hemp and bamboo textiles**: Unlike conventional cotton or synthetic fabrics, hemp and bamboo require less water, grow quickly, and regenerate soil.
- **Mushroom-based packaging**: Mycelium, the root structure of fungi, is being used to create biodegradable packaging materials, reducing plastic waste.
- **Bio-adhesives and bio-coatings**: Derived from plant oils and proteins, these replace synthetic adhesives that contribute to chemical pollution.

Adopting bio-based materials reduces reliance on finite fossil resources while closing the loop on biological resource cycles.

Ecosystem-Based Resource Management for Long-Term Sustainability

Sustainable biological resource use is not only about responsible extraction but also about maintaining ecosystem health and resilience. Ecosystem-based resource management (EBRM) ensures that landscapes, forests, fisheries, and wetlands continue to provide ecological services while supporting human needs.

Ecosystem-Based Resource Management Strategies:

- **Reforestation and afforestation projects**: Planting trees in degraded areas restores carbon sequestration, water regulation, and biodiversity.
- **Sustainable watershed management**: Protecting wetlands, river basins, and aquifers ensures clean water availability and prevents soil erosion.

- **Biodiversity-friendly land use planning**: Allocating land for wildlife corridors and conservation zones balances economic development with ecosystem protection.
- **Carbon farming and agroforestry**: Practices such as silvopasture and regenerative grazing integrate trees with agriculture to enhance carbon sequestration and soil fertility.

By adopting ecosystem-based approaches, industries and communities can use biological resources sustainably while safeguarding ecosystems for future generations.

Restoring Habitats Through Bio-Based Innovation

Ecosystems worldwide have been severely impacted by deforestation, urban expansion, industrial activities, and unsustainable resource extraction, leading to habitat loss and declining biodiversity. Conventional habitat restoration efforts often rely on mechanical interventions, such as large-scale replanting or engineered structures, which may not always align with natural ecosystem functions.

A circular bioeconomy approach to habitat restoration leverages bio-based innovations, integrating natural materials, biological processes, and regenerative technologies to rehabilitate degraded environments. These approaches prioritize ecosystem resilience, biodiversity recovery, and sustainable resource use, ensuring that restored habitats can self-sustain and adapt to changing environmental conditions.

This section explores bio-based innovations for habitat restoration, including biodegradable materials, bioengineered ecosystem restoration techniques, microbial solutions, and circular reforestation strategies that enhance long-term ecological health.

Biodegradable and Bio-Based Materials for Habitat Restoration

Traditional habitat restoration projects often rely on synthetic materials, such as plastic tree guards or concrete barriers, which can cause long-term environmental pollution. Bio-based alternatives offer sustainable, biodegradable solutions that integrate into natural landscapes without leaving harmful residues.

Bio-Based Restoration Materials:

- **Mycelium-based erosion control**: Fungal mycelium mats reinforce soil, preventing erosion and landslides while enhancing soil microbiology.
- **Biodegradable tree guards**: Made from plant fibers and bio-polymers, these decompose naturally as trees mature, eliminating plastic waste.
- **Bio-based reef structures**: Artificial reefs made from calcium carbonate and natural minerals provide marine habitat restoration while supporting coral growth.
- **Seed-embedded biodegradable textiles**: Fabric mats infused with native plant seeds promote revegetation in degraded landscapes without requiring artificial fertilizers.

By using biodegradable materials, restoration projects can accelerate ecosystem recovery while reducing environmental impact.

Bioengineered Solutions for Ecosystem Regeneration

Advances in biotechnology and genetic science are opening new possibilities for restoring ecosystems through bioengineering techniques. These solutions utilize enhanced plant species, microbes, and regenerative organisms to revitalize degraded landscapes.

Key Bioengineered Restoration Techniques:

- **Microbial-assisted soil recovery**: Beneficial microbes, such as nitrogen-fixing bacteria and mycorrhizal fungi, improve soil fertility and plant resilience in degraded areas.

- **Bioengineered wetlands for water filtration**: Wetland plants enhanced with water-purifying microbes remove toxins from contaminated water bodies.
- **CRISPR-enhanced native species**: Genetic modification of drought-resistant trees and salt-tolerant plants supports restoration in climate-vulnerable ecosystems.
- **Living shorelines with bioengineered seagrasses**: Using lab-grown seagrasses accelerates coastal habitat restoration, protecting against erosion and rising sea levels.

By integrating bioengineering and ecological restoration, degraded habitats can recover faster, more effectively, and with greater resilience to climate change.

Microbial and Bio-Remediation Approaches

Many degraded habitats suffer from soil contamination, water pollution, and nutrient depletion, making natural regeneration difficult. Microbial and bio-remediation techniques harness the power of bacteria, fungi, and other microorganisms to detoxify and restore damaged ecosystems.

Circular Microbial Restoration Methods:

- **Bioremediation of polluted soils**: Oil-degrading bacteria break down hydrocarbons in contaminated industrial sites, restoring soil quality.
- **Mycoremediation with fungi**: Mycelium networks absorb heavy metals, pesticides, and other pollutants from degraded land and waterways.
- **Probiotic restoration of coral reefs**: Beneficial bacterial strains introduced to corals improve resilience against bleaching and ocean acidification.
- **Algae-based carbon capture**: Fast-growing algae species absorb excess carbon dioxide and restore aquatic ecosystems affected by climate change.

By using microbial-based restoration methods, polluted habitats can be rehabilitated naturally and effectively without excessive reliance on chemical treatments.

Circular Reforestation and Landscape Regeneration

Traditional reforestation efforts often focus on mass tree planting, but without holistic land management, these initiatives may fail to restore full ecosystem functions. A circular bioeconomy approach ensures that reforestation efforts integrate biodiversity, soil regeneration, and sustainable resource cycles.

Circular Reforestation Strategies:

- **Miyawaki forests**: A method of planting dense, fast-growing mini-forests using native species to accelerate ecological succession.
- **Assisted natural regeneration (ANR)**: Protecting naturally sprouting seedlings rather than replanting new trees allows ecosystems to recover with minimal human intervention.
- **Multi-species agroforestry**: Blending trees, crops, and livestock creates self-sustaining landscapes that provide economic benefits while restoring biodiversity.
- **Seed dispersal using drones and animals**: Aerial and animal-assisted seed distribution helps restore large-scale degraded landscapes efficiently.

By applying circular principles to reforestation, landscapes can recover more effectively while ensuring long-term environmental and economic benefits.

Biodiversity Conservation Through Circular Supply Chains

Biodiversity is essential for ecosystem stability, food security, and climate resilience, yet conventional linear supply chains often contribute to deforestation, habitat destruction, and overexploitation of natural resources. The extraction, production, and disposal of goods in a take-make-waste system leads to land degradation, pollution, and loss of species diversity. Unsustainable supply chains drive unsustainable land use, excessive water consumption, and high carbon emissions, further straining fragile ecosystems.

A circular supply chain ensures that resources are used efficiently, waste is minimized, and biodiversity is protected by keeping materials in use for as long as possible. By integrating sustainable sourcing, regenerative practices, closed-loop production, and ethical consumer choices, circular supply chains reduce environmental harm while supporting ecosystem restoration.

This section explores how circular supply chains contribute to biodiversity conservation, focusing on sustainable sourcing, regenerative production models, waste reduction strategies, and ethical business practices.

Sustainable Sourcing to Protect Ecosystems

Many industries rely on natural raw materials, such as timber, minerals, and agricultural commodities, but unsustainable extraction leads to deforestation, soil depletion, and biodiversity loss. A circular approach to sourcing prioritizes ecosystem health by ensuring that materials are harvested responsibly, replenished, and certified as sustainable.

Circular Sourcing Strategies for Biodiversity Conservation:

- **Certified sustainable products**: Supporting FSC-certified timber, organic cotton, and Rainforest Alliance-certified coffee ensures that products come from responsibly managed ecosystems.
- **Deforestation-free supply chains**: Companies commit to zero-deforestation policies, sourcing materials only from lands that have not been recently cleared.

- **Regenerative agriculture sourcing**: Prioritizing suppliers that use agroforestry, cover cropping, and natural fertilizers helps restore soil health and reduce biodiversity loss.
- **Ethical wild harvesting**: Ensuring that medicinal plants, seafood, and non-timber forest products are harvested sustainably prevents species depletion and habitat destruction.

By adopting sustainable sourcing strategies, businesses can support biodiversity while ensuring long-term resource availability.

Regenerative Production Models for Biodiversity-Friendly Farming and Manufacturing

Traditional agricultural and manufacturing practices often degrade ecosystems through monocropping, chemical pollution, and habitat destruction. Regenerative production models integrate circular economy principles to restore soils, waterways, and forests, enhancing biodiversity.

Biodiversity-Friendly Production Strategies:

- **Agroecology and diversified farming**: Growing a mix of crops and incorporating trees, shrubs, and wildlife corridors supports pollinators, soil organisms, and native species.
- **Circular aquaculture**: Using low-impact fish farming techniques, such as integrated multi-trophic aquaculture (IMTA), reduces water pollution while maintaining marine biodiversity.
- **Biodegradable and eco-friendly production materials**: Using plant-based plastics, organic dyes, and compostable packaging reduces the harmful impact of synthetic materials on ecosystems.
- **Nature-positive textile production**: Shifting from synthetic fibers to regenerative fibers, such as hemp, bamboo, and mycelium-based materials, reduces chemical runoff and land degradation.

By implementing regenerative production methods, industries can contribute to ecosystem restoration while reducing their ecological footprint.

Waste Reduction and Resource Efficiency to Protect Natural Habitats

Waste from industrial and consumer activities often ends up in landfills or natural environments, contaminating soil and water, harming wildlife, and reducing habitat quality. Circular supply chains prioritize waste minimization, reuse, and recycling, preventing biodiversity loss caused by pollution and excessive resource extraction.

Circular Waste Reduction Strategies:

- **Product life extension**: Designing modular, repairable, and upgradable products reduces the demand for raw materials, lowering pressure on forests, fisheries, and natural habitats.
- **Closed-loop manufacturing**: Implementing zero-waste production processes ensures that byproducts and excess materials are repurposed rather than discarded.
- **Industrial symbiosis**: One company's waste becomes another's raw material (e.g., using brewery grain waste to produce bio-based packaging).
- **Plastics and chemical reduction**: Phasing out non-recyclable plastics and toxic chemicals prevents pollution that harms marine and terrestrial ecosystems.

Reducing waste through circular supply chains protects biodiversity by reducing pollution, minimizing habitat destruction, and conserving resources.

Ethical Consumer Choices and Corporate Responsibility

Biodiversity conservation is not just the responsibility of producers—it requires consumer awareness and corporate accountability to create market demand for sustainable products. Ethical consumption and corporate sustainability commitments can drive the transition to biodiversity-friendly supply chains.

How Ethical Choices Support Biodiversity Conservation:

- **Eco-labeling and transparent supply chains**: Consumers choose products with certifications like Fair Trade, MSC (Marine Stewardship Council), and organic labels, supporting ethical sourcing.
- **Circular business models**: Companies shifting to subscription-based, product-as-a-service, and resale platforms reduce demand for virgin raw materials.
- **Biodiversity-positive investments**: Businesses and investors prioritize projects that restore forests, protect endangered species, and support regenerative agriculture.
- **Regenerative corporate policies**: Companies commit to nature-based solutions, habitat restoration, and responsible land use planning in their operations.

Through consumer advocacy and corporate responsibility, circular supply chains can support biodiversity conservation while promoting sustainable economic growth.

Harnessing Nature's Regenerative Potential for Ecosystem Services

Ecosystems provide essential services that support life on Earth, including clean air and water, carbon sequestration, soil fertility, and climate regulation. However, human activities such as deforestation, urban expansion, and industrial pollution have disrupted these natural systems, reducing their ability to function effectively. The loss of forests, wetlands, grasslands, and biodiversity has weakened ecosystems, making them more vulnerable to climate change, extreme weather events, and resource depletion.

A circular approach to ecosystem management focuses on harnessing nature's regenerative potential to restore and enhance ecosystem services. By working with natural processes rather than against them, we can accelerate ecological recovery, increase biodiversity, and build resilience in human and natural systems.

This section explores key strategies for leveraging nature's regenerative power, including soil regeneration, water cycle restoration, carbon sequestration through reforestation, and biodiversity-driven ecosystem services.

Soil Regeneration to Enhance Land Productivity and Resilience

Soil is one of the most valuable yet often overlooked natural assets. Healthy soils store carbon, retain water, and support plant and microbial life, ensuring the sustainability of food systems and landscapes. However, unsustainable land use, intensive agriculture, and erosion have degraded vast areas of soil, reducing their ability to support life and regulate the environment.

Regenerative Soil Management Practices:

- **Cover cropping and green manure**: Planting cover crops like clover and legumes restores soil nutrients, improves moisture retention, and prevents erosion.
- **Minimal tillage and soil conservation farming**: Reducing soil disturbance protects beneficial microbes and preserves soil structure, enhancing long-term fertility.
- **Organic soil amendments**: Compost, biochar, and manure enrich the soil, replenishing lost nutrients and increasing carbon sequestration.
- **Agroforestry and silvopasture**: Integrating trees into agricultural landscapes stabilizes soil, improves water retention, and supports biodiversity.

By restoring degraded soils, we can increase agricultural productivity, enhance ecosystem resilience, and improve carbon storage capacity.

Restoring the Water Cycle Through Nature-Based Solutions

Water is a fundamental resource for life, but overuse, pollution, and climate change have disrupted the natural water cycle, leading to droughts, floods, and declining freshwater availability. Harnessing nature's ability to regulate water can improve water security, restore aquatic ecosystems, and reduce the impact of extreme weather events.

Nature-Based Water Management Strategies:

- **Wetland restoration**: Rehabilitating wetlands filters pollutants, stores excess rainfall, and replenishes groundwater, helping regulate the water cycle.
- **Reforestation for watershed protection**: Trees and vegetation prevent runoff and erosion, ensuring steady water availability for rivers and aquifers.
- **Green infrastructure in cities**: Permeable pavements, green roofs, and rain gardens reduce urban water runoff and increase natural filtration.
- **Decentralized rainwater harvesting**: Collecting and storing rainwater supports community resilience and reduces reliance on centralized water supplies.

By restoring water systems using natural solutions, we can secure clean water supplies, reduce flood risks, and support healthy aquatic ecosystems.

Carbon Sequestration Through Reforestation and Regenerative Landscapes

Forests and other vegetated landscapes act as carbon sinks, absorbing and storing carbon dioxide from the atmosphere.

However, deforestation and land degradation have significantly reduced the planet's ability to regulate carbon levels, contributing to climate change. Regenerating forests and grasslands helps capture atmospheric carbon, mitigating global warming while restoring ecosystem functions.

Key Strategies for Carbon Sequestration:

- **Rewilding and afforestation**: Planting native species and allowing ecosystems to regenerate naturally enhances carbon storage and biodiversity.
- **Regenerative grazing and pasture management**: Managing livestock in ways that promote grass growth and soil carbon storage supports climate resilience.
- **Mangrove and coastal ecosystem restoration**: Coastal vegetation, such as mangroves and seagrasses, sequester carbon at higher rates than terrestrial forests while protecting coastlines.
- **Urban reforestation and green spaces**: Expanding green spaces in cities absorbs CO_2, improves air quality, and enhances urban cooling.

By prioritizing carbon sequestration through ecosystem restoration, we can combat climate change while enhancing biodiversity and ecosystem health.

Biodiversity-Driven Ecosystem Services

Biodiversity underpins ecosystem services, supporting everything from pollination and natural pest control to climate adaptation and food security. However, biodiversity loss due to habitat destruction, pollution, and climate change has weakened many ecosystems, reducing their ability to provide essential services.

Biodiversity-Based Ecosystem Service Strategies:

- **Pollinator-friendly agriculture**: Protecting bees, butterflies, and other pollinators enhances crop yields and ecosystem resilience.
- **Natural pest management**: Encouraging predator species, such as birds and beneficial insects, reduces the need for chemical pesticides.
- **Wildlife corridors and habitat restoration**: Connecting fragmented habitats allows species to migrate and adapt to environmental changes, strengthening ecosystem stability.
- **Regenerative ocean and marine conservation**: Restoring coral reefs, kelp forests, and marine protected areas improves fisheries, coastal protection, and carbon storage.

By preserving and enhancing biodiversity, we ensure that ecosystems continue to provide crucial services that sustain life and economic activities.

Chapter 7: Sustainable Infrastructure and the Built Environment

The built environment plays a crucial role in shaping human societies, but conventional infrastructure development often leads to resource depletion, high carbon emissions, and habitat destruction. Traditional construction practices rely heavily on linear resource use, where materials are extracted, used, and discarded, contributing to waste accumulation, energy inefficiency, and environmental degradation.

A circular approach to infrastructure integrates sustainable materials, resource efficiency, and nature-based solutions to minimize environmental impact while ensuring long-term resilience. By designing buildings, cities, and infrastructure with circularity in mind, societies can reduce waste, improve energy efficiency, and enhance urban sustainability.

This chapter explores key strategies for sustainable infrastructure and the built environment, including circular construction materials, green building design, urban regeneration, and nature-based infrastructure solutions. Transitioning to a circular built environment is essential for reducing environmental footprints, improving climate resilience, and fostering more sustainable cities and communities.

Circular Materials and Construction Methods

The construction industry is one of the largest consumers of natural resources and generates significant amounts of waste, greenhouse gas emissions, and environmental degradation. Traditional building materials, such as concrete, steel, and plastics, require extensive energy to produce and often result in high levels of waste at the end of their life cycle. The linear approach to construction—where materials are extracted, used, and discarded—creates long-term sustainability challenges.

A circular approach to construction focuses on reducing resource consumption, maximizing material reuse, and minimizing waste. By utilizing sustainable materials, designing for adaptability, and implementing closed-loop construction methods, infrastructure can become more resilient, energy-efficient, and environmentally responsible.

This section explores key circular strategies in construction, including sustainable building materials, modular and prefabricated construction, adaptive reuse of materials, and waste-reducing construction techniques.

Sustainable and Low-Impact Building Materials

Traditional construction materials, such as concrete and steel, have high carbon footprints due to energy-intensive production processes. Shifting to bio-based, recycled, and low-impact materials reduces environmental impact while maintaining structural integrity.

Circular Construction Materials:

- **Recycled concrete and reclaimed steel**: Instead of producing new concrete and steel, recycled materials from demolished buildings can be repurposed, reducing resource extraction.
- **Cross-laminated timber (CLT) and engineered wood**: Sustainably sourced wood products store carbon and provide structurally sound alternatives to steel and concrete.
- **Hempcrete and mycelium-based insulation**: Bio-based materials, such as hempcrete (hemp + lime) and mycelium (fungal root structures), offer lightweight, energy-efficient, and biodegradable alternatives.
- **Recycled plastics and glass**: Used plastics and glass can be transformed into durable construction materials, reducing landfill waste and promoting circularity.

By prioritizing circular materials, construction projects can lower their environmental footprint while promoting resource efficiency.

Modular and Prefabricated Construction for Resource Efficiency

Traditional construction generates excessive waste, delays, and energy consumption, whereas modular and prefabricated building techniques minimize material waste, optimize efficiency, and allow for future adaptability.

Advantages of Modular Construction:

- **Precision manufacturing**: Prefabrication in controlled environments reduces material waste compared to on-site construction.
- **Reuse and disassembly**: Modular structures can be easily deconstructed and repurposed, extending their lifespan.
- **Lower energy consumption**: Prefabricated materials require less energy for transportation and assembly, reducing the project's carbon footprint.
- **Scalability and flexibility**: Modular components allow buildings to be expanded, modified, or relocated, adapting to changing needs.

By adopting modular and prefabricated techniques, construction projects can achieve greater sustainability, cost efficiency, and design flexibility.

Adaptive Reuse and Circular Building Design

Rather than demolishing and rebuilding, adaptive reuse extends the life of existing buildings and materials, reducing demand for new resource extraction and minimizing waste.

Key Principles of Adaptive Reuse:

- **Repurposing old buildings for new functions**: Converting warehouses into offices, or former industrial sites into residential and commercial spaces, preserves embodied energy and reduces material waste.
- **Designing for disassembly (DfD)**: Buildings are designed to be easily deconstructed and their materials repurposed, ensuring long-term circularity.
- **Flexible and multi-use spaces**: Creating adaptable interiors and structures allows buildings to serve multiple purposes over time without requiring extensive renovations.
- **Preserving heritage structures**: Restoring older buildings instead of replacing them conserves cultural and historical value while reducing construction emissions.

Adaptive reuse supports a circular economy by prolonging material life cycles and minimizing environmental impact.

Waste Reduction and Closed-Loop Construction Techniques

A circular approach to construction prioritizes waste minimization and material recovery, ensuring that building materials are reused, recycled, or repurposed instead of being discarded.

Circular Waste Reduction Strategies:

- **Deconstruction over demolition**: Instead of demolishing old buildings, components such as bricks, doors, and windows can be salvaged and reused.
- **On-site material recycling**: Using crushed concrete and reclaimed wood for new projects reduces waste and promotes circularity.
- **Smart material tracking systems**: Digital tools, such as Building Information Modeling (BIM), help track material use, reducing overproduction and optimizing reuse.
- **Circular concrete solutions**: Innovations like self-healing concrete and geopolymer concrete reduce the need for energy-intensive cement production.

By eliminating construction waste and ensuring materials remain in circulation, the industry can transition towards a zero-waste, sustainable future.

Integrating Nature into Urban and Industrial Spaces

Urbanization and industrial expansion have traditionally prioritized built environments over natural ecosystems, leading to biodiversity loss, air and water pollution, and increased vulnerability to climate change. Conventional urban and industrial development often neglects green infrastructure, natural water management, and biodiversity conservation, resulting in heat islands, poor air quality, and reduced resilience to extreme weather events.

A circular approach to urban and industrial spaces integrates natural elements into infrastructure design, ensuring that cities and industrial areas work in harmony with nature rather than against it. By incorporating green spaces, water-sensitive design, urban forests, and industrial ecology principles, built environments can become more resilient, sustainable, and livable.

This section explores key strategies for integrating nature into cities and industrial areas, including urban green spaces, nature-based solutions for water management, green roofs and facades, and circular industrial ecosystems.

Expanding Urban Green Spaces for Climate Resilience

Urban green spaces, including parks, tree-lined streets, and community gardens, provide essential ecosystem services that enhance air quality, biodiversity, and climate resilience. Expanding natural elements in urban settings helps mitigate the effects of pollution, extreme temperatures, and urban sprawl.

Key Benefits of Urban Green Spaces:

- **Cooling urban areas**: Trees and vegetation reduce heat island effects, lowering temperatures and improving thermal comfort.
- **Improving air quality**: Green spaces filter particulate matter, CO_2, and pollutants, enhancing overall air quality.
- **Supporting biodiversity**: Parks and green corridors provide habitats for birds, pollinators, and native species, strengthening urban biodiversity.
- **Enhancing mental and physical health**: Access to natural environments in cities promotes well-being, recreation, and social cohesion.

By prioritizing urban greenery, cities can become more livable and environmentally sustainable while fostering resilient ecosystems.

Nature-Based Solutions for Sustainable Water Management

Urban and industrial areas generate significant stormwater runoff, wastewater, and pollution, putting stress on natural water systems. Conventional water management relies on concrete drainage systems that often fail to capture and filter water efficiently. NbS help regulate water flow, improve quality, and restore hydrological balance.

Water Management Strategies Using Nature-Based Solutions:

- **Permeable pavements**: Reducing runoff by allowing rainwater to filter through surfaces, replenishing groundwater.
- **Constructed wetlands**: Engineered wetlands naturally filter pollutants from wastewater, improving water quality before discharge.
- **Bioswales and rain gardens**: These green infrastructure features capture stormwater, reduce flooding, and enhance urban aesthetics.

- **Restored riverbanks and floodplains**: Protecting urban waterways with vegetation and wetlands improves ecosystem health and water retention.

By integrating nature-based water management, cities and industrial zones can enhance resilience to floods, droughts, and water pollution.

Green Roofs, Vertical Gardens, and Living Facades

Buildings and industrial complexes contribute significantly to urban heat islands and energy consumption. Green roofs, vertical gardens, and living facades are innovative solutions that integrate plant life directly into buildings, reducing energy demand, enhancing air quality, and supporting biodiversity.

Circular Benefits of Green Infrastructure in Buildings:

- **Thermal regulation**: Green roofs and facades insulate buildings, reducing energy consumption for heating and cooling.
- **Stormwater absorption**: Green roofs capture rainwater, preventing excess runoff and urban flooding.
- **Air purification**: Vertical gardens absorb carbon dioxide and pollutants, improving urban air quality.
- **Wildlife habitat creation**: Green facades and rooftop gardens provide habitats for birds, pollinators, and beneficial insects.

By adopting green infrastructure, urban and industrial developments can reduce their environmental footprint while creating healthier, more sustainable spaces.

Circular Industrial Ecosystems: Closing Resource Loops in Production Zones

Industrial areas are traditionally resource-intensive and waste-generating, but circular industrial ecosystems integrate nature-inspired principles to create self-sustaining, low-waste production networks. These models emphasize closed-loop material flows, industrial symbiosis, and eco-industrial parks that reduce pollution and enhance sustainability.

Key Circular Strategies for Industrial Integration with Nature:

- **Industrial symbiosis**: Waste from one factory becomes a resource for another, reducing raw material demand and emissions.
- **Eco-industrial parks**: Clusters of industries share resources, energy, and byproducts, optimizing efficiency.
- **Bioremediation in industrial areas**: Microorganisms and plants are used to clean contaminated soils and waterways near factories.
- **Renewable energy integration**: Solar, wind, and biogas energy systems power industrial zones, reducing fossil fuel dependence.

By transitioning to circular industrial systems, manufacturing zones can minimize waste, regenerate ecosystems, and operate more sustainably.

The Role of Green Infrastructure in Circular Cities

As urban populations grow and climate challenges intensify, cities must transition to sustainable, resilient models that balance economic development with environmental conservation. Traditional urban infrastructure, characterized by concrete-dominated landscapes, high energy consumption, and linear resource use, often depletes natural resources and exacerbates climate-related vulnerabilities such as flooding, heat stress, and air pollution.

A circular city integrates green infrastructure to enhance resource efficiency, biodiversity, and climate resilience while reducing waste and pollution. Green infrastructure refers to nature-based solutions that incorporate vegetation, water management systems, and ecological restoration into urban planning. Unlike conventional infrastructure, which follows a linear approach of consumption and disposal, green infrastructure closes resource loops by mimicking natural cycles, recycling nutrients, capturing carbon, and improving urban ecosystems.

This section explores the role of green infrastructure in circular cities, focusing on multifunctional urban landscapes, stormwater management, energy-efficient buildings, and climate-adaptive design.

Multifunctional Urban Landscapes for Resilient Cities

Green infrastructure in circular cities is multifunctional, serving multiple ecological and social purposes simultaneously. Instead of single-purpose infrastructure (e.g., roads, parking lots), multifunctional landscapes integrate greenery into public spaces, enhancing urban resilience.

Key Green Infrastructure Strategies:

- **Urban forests and tree canopies**: Trees reduce urban heat island effects, filter pollutants, and sequester carbon.
- **Green corridors and wildlife-friendly parks**: Expanding green spaces promotes biodiversity, supports pollinators, and improves air quality.
- **Mixed-use public spaces**: Parks and plazas incorporate water management features, shaded walkways, and community gathering spaces.
- **Edible landscapes and community gardens**: Urban farming and food forests enhance food security while reducing carbon footprints.

By designing multifunctional urban landscapes, cities can optimize land use, enhance ecosystem services, and create healthier living environments.

Green Stormwater Management and Circular Water Systems

Conventional stormwater systems rely on hard infrastructure, such as drains and pipes, which often lead to water runoff pollution, sewer overflows, and inefficient water use. Green stormwater management integrates natural filtration systems that absorb, store, and reuse rainwater, contributing to circular water cycles.

Circular Water Management Solutions:

- **Bioswales and rain gardens**: These natural filtration systems capture stormwater runoff, preventing pollution in rivers and lakes.
- **Permeable pavements**: Unlike traditional asphalt, these surfaces allow rainwater to infiltrate the ground, replenishing aquifers.
- **Constructed wetlands**: Artificial wetlands act as biological treatment plants, filtering wastewater before it re-enters the ecosystem.
- **Rainwater harvesting systems**: Collecting and storing rainwater for non-potable uses, such as irrigation and cooling, reduces demand on municipal supplies.

By integrating nature-based water solutions, circular cities can improve water security, reduce flooding risks, and enhance urban climate resilience.

Green Buildings and Energy-Efficient Urban Design

Green infrastructure extends beyond landscapes into building design, incorporating renewable energy, natural cooling systems, and material reuse to reduce environmental impact. Circular building principles ensure that infrastructure is energy-efficient, adaptable, and minimizes resource waste.

Sustainable Urban Building Strategies:

- **Green roofs and living walls**: These features insulate buildings, reduce cooling costs, and absorb air pollutants.
- **Solar-integrated rooftops**: Harnessing solar energy for power generation contributes to self-sufficient energy systems.
- **Passive design principles**: Buildings oriented for natural ventilation and daylighting lower energy demands.
- **Recycled and bio-based materials**: Using reclaimed wood, bamboo, and mycelium-based insulation reduces carbon-intensive material consumption.

By adopting green and energy-efficient building designs, cities can lower their carbon footprint while improving indoor and outdoor air quality.

Climate-Adaptive Infrastructure and Disaster Resilience

Climate change is increasing the frequency of extreme weather events, including heatwaves, storms, and sea-level rise. Green infrastructure plays a critical role in adapting cities to these challenges by providing natural flood barriers, urban cooling systems, and disaster-resilient landscapes.

Climate-Resilient Green Infrastructure Strategies:

- **Mangroves and coastal wetlands**: These natural buffers protect cities from storm surges and coastal erosion.
- **Heat-reflective urban landscapes**: Using vegetation and reflective surfaces lowers city temperatures, reducing heat stress.

- **Nature-based flood mitigation**: Expanding floodplains, riverbank vegetation, and sponge cities enhances water absorption capacity.
- **Integrated blue-green infrastructure**: Combining urban water systems with vegetation improves climate resilience while enhancing biodiversity.

By prioritizing climate-adaptive green infrastructure, circular cities become more resilient to climate disruptions and ecological degradation.

Adaptive Reuse and Retrofitting for a Circular Built Environment

The built environment is one of the largest contributors to resource consumption, carbon emissions, and waste generation. Traditional urban development follows a linear model, where buildings are constructed, used, and eventually demolished, leading to high levels of material waste, energy loss, and environmental degradation. However, a circular approach to construction and urban development prioritizes adaptive reuse and retrofitting, extending the lifespan of existing buildings, reducing the need for new materials, and enhancing urban sustainability.

Adaptive reuse involves repurposing old buildings for new uses, while retrofitting focuses on upgrading existing structures to improve energy efficiency, resilience, and functionality. These strategies help cities preserve architectural heritage, reduce demolition waste, and lower the environmental footprint of new construction.

This section explores key approaches to adaptive reuse and retrofitting, including structural rehabilitation, energy-efficient upgrades, material conservation, and smart urban redevelopment.

Extending Building Lifespan Through Structural Rehabilitation

Many older buildings face functional obsolescence due to outdated materials, poor insulation, or inefficient layouts. Rather than demolishing them, structural rehabilitation ensures that they remain safe, functional, and relevant to modern needs while preserving their embodied energy.

Structural Rehabilitation Strategies:

- **Foundation and framework strengthening**: Reinforcing walls, columns, and beams extends the structural integrity of aging buildings.
- **Seismic retrofitting**: Enhancing resilience to earthquakes and extreme weather ensures that structures remain viable.
- **Roof and facade restoration**: Upgrading roofs, windows, and exteriors prevents deterioration while improving energy efficiency.
- **Adaptive space conversion**: Repurposing warehouses into offices, cultural centers, or mixed-use developments maximizes urban land use.

By rehabilitating existing buildings, cities can reduce construction-related waste while maintaining historical and cultural continuity.

Energy-Efficient Retrofitting for Sustainable Urban Spaces

Older buildings often suffer from high energy consumption due to poor insulation, outdated HVAC systems, and inefficient lighting. Retrofitting improves energy performance, reducing operational costs and carbon emissions while promoting long-term sustainability.

Energy-Efficient Retrofitting Techniques:

- **High-performance insulation and glazing**: Adding double-glazed windows and thermal insulation reduces heating and cooling needs.

- **LED lighting and smart energy systems**: Replacing traditional lighting with energy-efficient LED bulbs and motion-sensor controls optimizes electricity use.
- **Solar panel integration**: Retrofitting rooftops with photovoltaic panels enables buildings to generate renewable energy.
- **Water efficiency upgrades**: Installing low-flow fixtures, rainwater harvesting systems, and greywater recycling reduces urban water consumption.

Retrofitting buildings with energy-efficient solutions supports the transition to low-carbon, circular cities while enhancing occupant comfort and affordability.

Material Conservation and Circular Resource Use

The demolition of buildings generates millions of tons of waste annually, much of which could be salvaged, recycled, or repurposed. Adaptive reuse and retrofitting emphasize material conservation, reducing the demand for virgin resources and supporting a circular construction industry.

Circular Material Reuse Strategies:

- **Deconstruction over demolition**: Carefully dismantling buildings allows for brick, wood, and steel reclamation, minimizing landfill waste.
- **Repurposed construction materials**: Reusing old timber, bricks, doors, and metal fixtures preserves resources while reducing costs.
- **Bio-based material retrofits**: Integrating hempcrete, bamboo, and recycled insulation enhances sustainability in older structures.
- **3D printing with recycled materials**: Additive manufacturing allows for on-demand, waste-free construction components.

By conserving and repurposing materials, adaptive reuse contributes to circular supply chains and reduces the environmental impact of construction activities.

Smart Urban Redevelopment for Circular Cities

Beyond individual buildings, adaptive reuse and retrofitting play a critical role in smart urban regeneration, transforming obsolete industrial zones, abandoned buildings, and underutilized spaces into vibrant, sustainable hubs.

Key Circular Urban Redevelopment Strategies:

- **Mixed-use developments**: Converting aging commercial buildings into residential, retail, and office spaces maximizes urban efficiency.
- **Green retrofits for industrial zones**: Upgrading factories and warehouses with green roofs, solar panels, and rainwater harvesting fosters sustainable industry.
- **Reclaiming public spaces**: Transforming vacant lots, old parking structures, and abandoned railways into green parks and pedestrian-friendly areas improves urban livability.
- **Heritage conservation districts**: Protecting historical buildings while integrating modern efficiency upgrades balances cultural preservation and sustainability.

By incorporating circular urban redevelopment strategies, cities can breathe new life into neglected areas while minimizing environmental and social costs.

Chapter 8: Policy and Governance for Circular Restoration

The successful transition to a circular economy for ecosystem restoration requires strong policy frameworks and effective governance structures. While businesses and communities play a crucial role in advancing circular practices, policy interventions and regulatory mechanisms are necessary to scale solutions, ensure compliance, and incentivize sustainable practices. Without clear policies, the adoption of circular restoration strategies may remain fragmented, limiting their potential impact.

Governments, international organizations, and local authorities must develop coordinated strategies that support waste reduction, resource efficiency, biodiversity conservation, and sustainable land management. This involves regulatory incentives, financial mechanisms, public-private partnerships, and international cooperation to promote circular restoration initiatives at local, national, and global levels.

This chapter explores key policy and governance approaches that enable circular ecosystem restoration, including regulatory frameworks, financial incentives, cross-sector collaboration, and monitoring systems. By aligning policy measures with circular economy principles, decision-makers can ensure long-term sustainability, resilience, and economic viability in restoration efforts.

Regulatory Frameworks Supporting Circular Ecosystem Restoration

The transition to a circular economy for ecosystem restoration requires well-defined regulatory frameworks that promote sustainable resource management, waste reduction, and biodiversity conservation. Without clear policies, circular restoration efforts risk fragmentation, inconsistent adoption, and limited impact.

Governments and international institutions play a crucial role in establishing legislation, standards, and enforcement mechanisms that support the widespread adoption of circular principles in environmental restoration.

Regulatory frameworks create clear guidelines and obligations for businesses, industries, and communities, ensuring that ecosystem restoration efforts align with circular economy objectives. These regulations prevent environmental degradation, incentivize resource efficiency, and set legal requirements for waste recovery, sustainable land use, and regenerative practices.

This section explores key regulatory mechanisms that support circular ecosystem restoration, including environmental laws, EPR, land-use policies, and global agreements on sustainability.

Environmental Laws and Circular Economy Legislation

Many governments have introduced environmental protection laws that integrate circular economy principles into land and resource management. These policies help enforce sustainable practices, reduce waste generation, and promote ecological restoration.

Examples of Environmental Laws Supporting Circular Restoration:

- **Circular economy legislation**: Policies that mandate waste reduction, material reuse, and eco-friendly production to prevent environmental harm.
- **Land restoration and conservation laws**: Legal frameworks requiring industries and developers to restore degraded ecosystems after resource extraction or land use.
- **Polluter-pays principle (PPP)**: Regulations that hold businesses accountable for environmental damage, requiring them to finance restoration and pollution mitigation efforts.

- **Zero-waste policies**: Bans on landfilling certain materials, encouraging recycling, composting, and remanufacturing to close resource loops.

By implementing strong environmental regulations, governments create legal obligations for industries and municipalities to adopt circular restoration practices.

EPR for Resource Management

EPR policies shift the burden of waste management from consumers and governments to manufacturers and producers. These frameworks encourage industries to design products with recyclability and reuse in mind, ensuring that materials stay within the economy rather than becoming waste.

How EPR Supports Circular Ecosystem Restoration:

- **Waste reduction and recycling obligations**: Companies must take responsibility for collecting, processing, and repurposing materials at the end of their lifecycle.
- **Incentives for eco-friendly design**: Producers are encouraged to develop biodegradable, recyclable, or reusable materials to minimize environmental impact.
- **Resource recovery targets**: Governments set specific waste diversion and recycling benchmarks, requiring businesses to adopt circular strategies.
- **Deposit-return schemes**: Consumers return used materials (e.g., plastics, electronics, packaging) for remanufacturing or responsible disposal.

EPR regulations reduce landfill waste, conserve natural resources, and create financial incentives for companies to participate in circular restoration efforts.

Land-Use and Biodiversity Protection Policies

Sustainable land-use policies are essential for preventing ecosystem degradation and promoting circular restoration initiatives. Governments can establish zoning laws, protected area regulations, and ecological restoration mandates that prioritize sustainable development and conservation.

Key Land-Use and Biodiversity Protection Policies:

- **Reforestation and afforestation mandates**: Requirements for industries to replant trees or restore landscapes after development projects.
- **Nature-based solutions in urban planning**: Green infrastructure laws that require green roofs, permeable pavements, and urban forests in city planning.
- **Biodiversity conservation regulations**: Policies that protect critical habitats and endangered species by restricting harmful land use.
- **Sustainable agriculture and soil protection laws**: Encouraging regenerative farming techniques that prevent soil degradation and nutrient loss.

By integrating land-use regulations with circular restoration strategies, governments ensure that ecosystems remain resilient and capable of regenerating naturally.

Global Agreements and Cross-Border Environmental Policies

Ecosystem restoration and circular economy adoption require global cooperation to address climate change, resource depletion, and environmental degradation. International agreements and cross-border policies help align national regulations with sustainability goals.

Examples of Global Agreements Supporting Circular Ecosystem Restoration:

- **The Paris Agreement**: Encourages countries to adopt climate-resilient land-use practices and invest in carbon sequestration projects.
- **The Kunming-Montreal Global Biodiversity Framework**: Aims to halt biodiversity loss and integrate circular economy solutions into environmental management.
- **The Basel Convention**: Regulates the international movement of hazardous waste, ensuring responsible disposal and recovery.
- **The UN Sustainable Development Goals (SDGs)**: Provide a roadmap for circular economy adoption in restoration, water management, and sustainable land use.

By aligning national policies with global frameworks, governments can collaborate on large-scale restoration initiatives, share best practices, and create cross-border circular economy solutions.

Incentives for Businesses and Communities

Transitioning to a circular economy for ecosystem restoration requires the active participation of both businesses and communities. However, without strong financial and regulatory incentives, many organizations and individuals may struggle to adopt sustainable practices. Governments and policymakers play a crucial role in creating incentives that encourage businesses and communities to invest in circular solutions, resource efficiency, and environmental restoration.

Incentives can take the form of financial support, tax benefits, market-based instruments, and regulatory advantages, ensuring that sustainable practices are both economically viable and socially beneficial. These mechanisms help shift economic priorities toward waste reduction, circular resource use, and long-term environmental sustainability.

This section explores key incentive structures that support businesses and communities in adopting circular ecosystem restoration practices, including financial incentives, tax benefits, certification programs, and community-based reward systems.

Financial Incentives and Grants for Circular Business Models

Many businesses hesitate to adopt circular economy practices due to upfront costs and financial risks. To address this, governments and financial institutions provide grants, low-interest loans, and investment incentives to support companies transitioning to sustainable production models.

Types of Financial Incentives for Businesses:

- **Green innovation grants**: Funding for R&D in circular solutions, such as biodegradable materials, renewable energy, and sustainable product design.
- **Low-interest loans for circular infrastructure**: Businesses investing in recycling facilities, sustainable packaging, or energy-efficient technologies can access preferential financing.
- **Public-private partnerships (PPPs)**: Governments collaborate with private companies to develop large-scale restoration projects, such as reforestation or water conservation initiatives.
- **Sustainability-linked loans**: Financial products with lower interest rates for businesses meeting environmental performance targets, such as reducing emissions or increasing material recovery rates.

By providing financial support, governments reduce the economic burden on businesses, making circular economy solutions more accessible and attractive.

Tax Benefits and Economic Incentives for Circular Practices

Taxation policies play a major role in shaping corporate behavior. Many governments use tax breaks, exemptions, and subsidies to encourage businesses to implement circular strategies and invest in ecosystem restoration.

Key Tax Incentives for Circular Economy Adoption:

- **Tax credits for eco-friendly investments**: Companies receive tax reductions for investing in renewable energy, recycling systems, and sustainable supply chains.
- **Landfill and resource extraction taxes**: Higher taxes on waste disposal and raw material extraction incentivize businesses to reduce waste and adopt circular sourcing strategies.
- **Depreciation incentives for green infrastructure**: Businesses installing energy-efficient equipment, water recycling systems, or sustainable construction materials benefit from faster depreciation rates.
- **Tax breaks for environmental restoration projects**: Businesses funding reforestation, wetland restoration, or biodiversity conservation can deduct expenses from taxable income.

By making sustainable choices financially beneficial, tax incentives help businesses transition to circular models while maintaining profitability.

Certification and Labeling Programs for Circular Products

Consumers are increasingly prioritizing sustainable products and services, but businesses need recognition and market differentiation to highlight their circular economy commitments. Certification and eco-labeling programs provide credibility and market advantages for companies that implement circular strategies.

Examples of Circular Economy Certifications:

- **Cradle to Cradle (C2C) Certification**: Recognizes products designed for reuse, recycling, and minimal environmental impact.
- **EU Ecolabel and ISO 14001 Certification**: Demonstrates compliance with strict environmental sustainability standards.
- **Fair Trade and Rainforest Alliance Certification**: Ensures sustainable sourcing of raw materials while promoting ethical business practices.
- **B Corp Certification**: Awards businesses that meet high standards of social and environmental performance, transparency, and accountability.

By participating in certification programs, businesses gain consumer trust, competitive advantages, and potential financial incentives from sustainable procurement policies.

Community-Based Reward Systems for Circular Practices

Engaging communities in circular ecosystem restoration is essential for long-term success. However, individuals and small businesses may lack the financial resources or motivation to adopt circular practices without reward-based incentives. Governments and local organizations have developed community-based incentive programs to encourage participation in waste reduction, conservation, and sustainable consumption.

Community Reward Programs Supporting Circularity:

- **Deposit-refund schemes**: Consumers receive financial incentives for returning used packaging, electronic waste, or recyclable materials.
- **Green rewards programs**: Residents who participate in waste reduction, composting, or tree-planting initiatives earn discounts on public transport, utility bills, or local services.

- **Eco-token and barter systems**: Local governments introduce sustainability credits that can be exchanged for community services, local produce, or green products.
- **Citizen science and volunteer incentives**: Volunteers contributing to reforestation, beach clean-ups, or biodiversity monitoring receive recognition, awards, or tax benefits.

By integrating community incentives, local governments and organizations increase public engagement in circular ecosystem restoration while fostering a culture of sustainability.

Global and Local Policies Promoting Circular Restoration

The adoption of circular economy principles in ecosystem restoration requires effective policy frameworks at both global and local levels. While international agreements set broad sustainability targets, local policies play a crucial role in implementing practical solutions that align with regional environmental, economic, and social conditions. A combination of global cooperation and localized policy action is essential for addressing resource efficiency, waste reduction, biodiversity protection, and climate resilience.

Policymakers at all levels must establish legally binding regulations, financial incentives, and governance structures that encourage businesses, industries, and communities to transition from a linear economic model to a regenerative, circular approach. This section explores key global and local policy mechanisms that drive circular ecosystem restoration efforts, including international agreements, national circular economy strategies, municipal regulations, and city-led initiatives.

International Agreements and Frameworks for Circular Restoration

Global agreements set overarching goals for sustainable development, climate action, and biodiversity conservation. These frameworks guide national and local governments in shaping policies that integrate circular economy principles into ecosystem restoration.

Key Global Policies and Agreements:

- **The Paris Agreement (2015)**: Encourages countries to implement nature-based solutions and invest in carbon sequestration projects such as afforestation and wetland restoration.
- **The Kunming-Montreal Global Biodiversity Framework (2022)**: Establishes global targets for biodiversity conservation, sustainable land use, and ecosystem restoration by 2030.
- **The United Nations SDGs**: SDG 12 (Responsible Consumption and Production) and SDG 15 (Life on Land) promote circular economy principles for resource efficiency and habitat protection.
- **The EU Green Deal and Circular Economy Action Plan**: Provides a roadmap for reducing waste, increasing material reuse, and integrating circular economy strategies into policy frameworks.

By aligning national policies with global agreements, countries ensure that circular restoration strategies are widely adopted and effectively implemented.

National Circular Economy Strategies for Ecosystem Restoration

At the national level, governments establish circular economy roadmaps to transition industries, businesses, and communities toward sustainable resource use and ecosystem restoration. These strategies outline legal requirements, incentives, and performance targets to ensure that economic activities minimize environmental impact.

Examples of National Circular Economy Strategies:

- **China's Circular Economy Promotion Law**: Mandates waste reduction, industrial symbiosis, and resource recovery initiatives to support environmental conservation.
- **Finland's Circular Economy Roadmap**: Prioritizes regenerative agriculture, sustainable forestry, and nature-based solutions for ecosystem resilience.
- **Japan's Sound Material-Cycle Society Plan**: Promotes waste prevention, material reuse, and closed-loop systems for industrial and municipal sectors.
- **Canada's Zero Plastic Waste Strategy**: Implements EPR laws and promotes biodegradable materials to protect ecosystems from plastic pollution.

By implementing national circular economy policies, governments ensure that industries and municipalities adopt sustainable practices that contribute to ecosystem restoration and climate resilience.

Municipal Regulations and City-Led Circular Initiatives

Cities and local governments play a crucial role in applying circular economy principles to urban planning, waste management, and green infrastructure development. Since cities are major centers of resource consumption and waste generation, local policies can significantly impact ecosystem restoration and sustainability efforts.

Key Circular Policies at the Municipal Level:

- **Zero-waste city policies**: Cities like San Francisco and Amsterdam implement waste separation, composting, and landfill diversion programs to enhance material recovery.
- **Green infrastructure mandates**: Municipal governments require new developments to incorporate green roofs, permeable pavements, and urban reforestation to improve ecosystem services.

- **Sustainable water management regulations**: Cities adopt nature-based flood prevention systems, water recycling infrastructure, and stormwater capture programs to reduce water stress.
- **Circular construction policies**: Local building codes encourage the use of reclaimed materials, modular building techniques, and deconstruction over demolition.

By localizing circular economy strategies, cities can implement scalable solutions that enhance resilience, reduce waste, and promote sustainable development.

Public-Private Partnerships and Community Engagement in Circular Restoration

Effective circular economy policies rely on collaboration between governments, businesses, and communities. PPPs and community-led initiatives drive investment in ecosystem restoration, circular infrastructure, and sustainable resource management.

Examples of Collaborative Circular Restoration Efforts:

- **Private sector investment in circular supply chains**: Companies partner with governments to develop closed-loop production models that reduce waste and resource extraction.
- **Community-driven recycling programs**: Local residents participate in waste collection, composting, and circular product exchanges, reducing landfill dependency.
- **Eco-restoration incentives for businesses**: Companies receive tax benefits for funding reforestation, habitat restoration, and biodiversity conservation projects.
- **Citizen science and participatory environmental monitoring**: Communities contribute to data collection on biodiversity loss, soil health, and water quality, supporting policy decisions.

By fostering collaboration between the public and private sectors, circular restoration initiatives become more effective, scalable, and socially inclusive.

The Role of Public-Private Partnerships in Circular Economy Governance

The transition to a circular economy for ecosystem restoration requires collaborative efforts between governments, businesses, and civil society. PPPs play a crucial role in bridging the gap between policy objectives and practical implementation, enabling the scaling of circular solutions through shared investment, expertise, and innovation.

Governments often face financial, technical, and operational challenges in implementing large-scale waste reduction, ecosystem restoration, and sustainable infrastructure projects. The private sector, on the other hand, has the technological capabilities, financial resources, and business-driven efficiency to accelerate circular economy initiatives. By working together, public and private entities can leverage their respective strengths to develop sustainable, cost-effective, and scalable solutions that support environmental and economic objectives.

This section explores the importance of PPPs in circular economy governance, focusing on funding mechanisms, innovation-driven collaboration, regulatory support, and case examples of successful partnerships.

Funding Mechanisms for Circular Economy Partnerships

Financing remains one of the biggest barriers to implementing circular economy projects, as they often require significant upfront investment before generating long-term benefits. PPPs help mobilize financial resources by combining public funding, private capital, and multilateral investment to support circular restoration initiatives.

Common Financing Models in Circular Economy PPPs:

- **Blended finance**: Governments provide seed funding or risk guarantees to encourage private investment in circular infrastructure projects such as recycling plants, green energy solutions, and nature-based restoration.
- **Green bonds and sustainability-linked loans**: These financial instruments attract private capital for waste-to-resource innovations, circular manufacturing, and regenerative agriculture.
- **Performance-based contracts**: Private companies receive funding based on measurable circular economy outcomes, such as waste diversion rates, ecosystem restoration progress, or material recovery efficiency.
- **Corporate social responsibility (CSR) investment**: Businesses fund circular restoration projects as part of their ESG commitments, supporting broader sustainability goals.

By sharing financial risks and benefits, PPPs help scale large-scale circular initiatives while reducing financial burdens on governments.

Innovation and Technology Collaboration in Circular Economy

Public-private partnerships drive technological advancements in circular economy governance by encouraging knowledge exchange, research investment, and co-development of innovative solutions. Governments set policy priorities, while the private sector provides the technological expertise and operational efficiency needed to implement these strategies.

Key Areas of Innovation in Circular PPPs:

- **Advanced waste recovery and recycling technologies**: Companies collaborate with municipalities to develop AI-driven sorting systems, bio-based recycling solutions, and chemical recovery methods.

- **Smart infrastructure and digitalization**: IoT-enabled smart grids, blockchain-based waste tracking, and data-driven circular supply chains improve resource efficiency and accountability.
- **Regenerative agriculture and sustainable land use**: Agribusinesses partner with governments to implement soil regeneration programs, circular food production, and closed-loop nutrient cycles.
- **Eco-friendly product design and material innovation**: Joint R&D efforts focus on biodegradable packaging, circular textiles, and modular construction techniques to reduce resource depletion.

By combining public regulatory oversight with private-sector innovation, PPPs accelerate market-driven circular economy solutions.

Regulatory Support and Policy Alignment in Circular PPPs

For PPPs to succeed, clear regulatory frameworks must provide legal certainty, risk management, and accountability measures to guide private-sector participation in circular economy governance. Governments play a critical role in removing policy barriers and creating an enabling environment for sustainable investment.

Regulatory Measures Supporting Circular PPPs:

- **EPR frameworks**: Companies are required to take responsibility for the lifecycle of their products, incentivizing product reuse, remanufacturing, and sustainable sourcing.
- **Incentives for circular business models**: Tax reductions, grants, and regulatory fast-tracking support companies investing in eco-innovation and waste reduction strategies.
- **Standardized circularity metrics and reporting**: Establishing measurement frameworks for circular performance ensures transparency and compliance with sustainability goals.

- **Public procurement policies favoring circular products**: Governments prioritize purchasing recycled, upcycled, and sustainably sourced materials, driving demand for circular solutions.

Strong regulatory alignment fosters confidence among investors and businesses, ensuring that circular economy partnerships operate effectively and equitably.

Successful Public-Private Partnerships in Circular Economy

Several cities and industries have successfully implemented PPPs that integrate circular economy principles into governance and infrastructure. These case examples demonstrate scalable models that can be replicated globally.

Examples of Circular PPP Successes:

- **Amsterdam's Circular City Initiative**: A collaboration between the municipal government, businesses, and research institutions to create a fully circular economy by 2050, including waste-to-resource strategies, circular construction policies, and digital material tracking.
- **Singapore's Zero Waste Masterplan**: Public and private investment in advanced recycling technologies, water reclamation plants, and sustainable urban planning has made Singapore a leader in circular resource management.
- **Ellen MacArthur Foundation Partnerships**: Major corporations such as Unilever, IKEA, and Danone have partnered with NGOs and governments to implement closed-loop supply chains, plastic waste reduction initiatives, and regenerative production models.
- **Industrial Symbiosis in Kalundborg, Denmark**: A pioneering circular industrial ecosystem where one company's waste becomes another's resource, reducing emissions and improving efficiency across multiple industries.

By fostering strategic collaborations, these PPPs demonstrate how governments and businesses can jointly drive circular transformation.

Chapter 9: Financing and Scaling Circular Restoration Efforts

Transitioning to a circular economy for ecosystem restoration requires significant financial investment and scalable solutions that can be implemented across regions and sectors. While the principles of circular restoration—such as waste reduction, resource efficiency, and regenerative practices—offer long-term environmental and economic benefits, many projects face financial barriers, limited funding mechanisms, and challenges in scaling successful initiatives.

Effective financing strategies ensure that governments, businesses, and communities can access the resources needed to implement circular restoration projects at scale. This includes public and private investment, innovative funding models, and impact-driven financial mechanisms that support sustainable practices. Additionally, developing scalable frameworks enables successful circular restoration efforts to be expanded, replicated, and integrated into policy and business models worldwide.

This chapter explores key approaches for funding and expanding circular restoration efforts, including investment models, public-private financing mechanisms, scalable business strategies, and the role of technology in supporting large-scale adoption. By aligning financial incentives with circular economy principles, societies can ensure that ecosystem restoration efforts are both economically viable and environmentally effective in the long run.

Innovative Financing Mechanisms for Circular Restoration

Financing plays a critical role in scaling circular economy initiatives for ecosystem restoration. Traditional funding models often prioritize short-term economic returns, making it challenging to secure investment for long-term sustainability projects. To drive widespread adoption of circular restoration practices, innovative financing mechanisms are needed to bridge the gap between environmental goals and economic feasibility.

Innovative financing mechanisms focus on mobilizing public and private capital, reducing financial risks, and aligning economic incentives with environmental sustainability. These mechanisms ensure that businesses, governments, and communities can participate in circular restoration efforts without facing overwhelming financial burdens.

This section explores key financial models and instruments that support circular restoration, including green bonds, sustainability-linked loans, impact investing, and blended finance.

Green Bonds for Funding Circular Restoration

Green bonds are fixed-income financial instruments specifically designed to fund projects that deliver environmental benefits. These bonds provide governments, municipalities, and companies with access to capital for sustainable infrastructure, reforestation, waste management, and water conservation initiatives.

Key Features of Green Bonds in Circular Restoration:

- **Capital for large-scale projects**: Governments and private entities can issue green bonds to fund reforestation, regenerative agriculture, and circular infrastructure.
- **Long-term investment in sustainability**: Investors benefit from stable returns, while funds are directed toward environmental protection and resource efficiency.
- **Transparency and accountability**: Green bond issuers must follow strict reporting requirements to ensure that funds are allocated to legitimate circular economy projects.
- **Growing investor demand**: Institutional investors are increasingly prioritizing sustainable finance, creating more opportunities for circular restoration projects.

By leveraging green bonds, stakeholders can access long-term, low-cost financing to implement and expand circular restoration initiatives.

Sustainability-Linked Loans and Performance-Based Financing

Sustainability-linked loans (SLLs) and performance-based financing models offer businesses and municipalities financial incentives for achieving circular economy targets. Unlike traditional loans, SLLs tie interest rates and repayment terms to environmental performance metrics, such as waste reduction, carbon sequestration, or circular material use.

How Sustainability-Linked Loans Support Circular Restoration:

- **Lower interest rates for meeting sustainability targets**: Borrowers receive financial benefits for implementing waste recovery, renewable energy, or resource-efficient practices.
- **Encourages continuous improvement**: Companies and governments integrate circular economy principles to maintain or enhance financial incentives.
- **Applicable to diverse sectors**: SLLs can finance industrial circularity, eco-friendly construction, sustainable farming, and pollution control projects.
- **Aligns financial goals with environmental impact**: Investors and lenders are increasingly prioritizing ESG performance, making circular restoration projects more attractive.

Sustainability-linked loans help drive behavioral and operational change, ensuring that businesses and municipalities adopt measurable circular economy solutions.

Impact Investing and Private Sector Participation

Impact investing channels private capital into projects that generate measurable environmental and social benefits alongside financial

135

returns. Investors, foundations, and financial institutions allocate capital to circular economy startups, regenerative industries, and community-led restoration initiatives.

Key Aspects of Impact Investing in Circular Restoration:

- **Focus on long-term ecological impact**: Investors fund initiatives that restore degraded ecosystems, reduce carbon emissions, and enhance biodiversity.
- **Scalable investment opportunities**: Impact investors support startups and businesses specializing in circular product design, waste-to-resource innovations, and sustainable supply chains.
- **Measurable sustainability outcomes**: Investments are assessed using ESG indicators, carbon reduction metrics, and biodiversity conservation benchmarks.
- **Blended finance opportunities**: Impact investing often combines public and private funds to de-risk investments in circular restoration.

By engaging private sector investors, impact investing ensures that circular economy projects receive the capital needed for innovation and growth.

Blended Finance for Scaling Circular Economy Initiatives

Blended finance is a mechanism that combines public, private, and philanthropic funding to support high-risk, early-stage circular economy projects. By sharing financial risks, blended finance enables scaling and replication of circular restoration initiatives.

How Blended Finance Supports Circular Restoration:

- **Reduces financial risk**: Governments or development banks provide initial funding or guarantees, encouraging private investment.

- **Leverages diverse funding sources**: Public funds, grants, and private capital are combined to support regenerative agriculture, circular manufacturing, and nature-based solutions.
- **Supports developing economies**: Many circular restoration projects in emerging markets lack financial backing; blended finance helps de-risk investment in these regions.
- **Encourages multi-sector collaboration**: Businesses, financial institutions, and governments align efforts to fund circular economy transition strategies.

Blended finance mobilizes large-scale investments by ensuring that financial and environmental goals are mutually reinforcing.

Scaling Solutions for Broader Impact

Implementing circular economy principles for ecosystem restoration requires solutions that are not only effective at a local level but also scalable for broader impact. While many successful circular initiatives exist, expanding these solutions to regional, national, and global levels remains a challenge due to financial, technical, and governance barriers. Ensuring that circular restoration efforts are adaptable, cost-effective, and widely applicable is essential for achieving long-term environmental and economic benefits.

Scaling circular solutions involves leveraging technology, fostering collaboration, creating enabling policies, and integrating financial support mechanisms. It requires the participation of governments, businesses, investors, and local communities to replicate successful models across different ecosystems, industries, and geographies.

This section explores key strategies for scaling circular economy restoration efforts, including technology-driven expansion, cross-sector collaboration, regulatory support, and community engagement.

Leveraging Technology for Scalable Circular Solutions

Technology plays a crucial role in scaling circular restoration efforts by enhancing efficiency, improving monitoring capabilities, and enabling data-driven decision-making. Digital solutions, automation, and smart systems make it possible to expand circular practices across industries and geographic regions.

Key Technological Enablers for Scaling Circular Economy Solutions:

- **Artificial Intelligence (AI) and Big Data**: AI-driven models analyze waste streams, material flows, and ecosystem restoration progress, optimizing resource use.
- **Blockchain for Circular Supply Chains**: Blockchain technology ensures transparent tracking of materials and resources, enabling responsible sourcing and waste recovery at scale.
- **IoT Sensors for Environmental Monitoring**: Internet of Things (IoT) devices track soil health, water quality, and pollution levels, helping optimize circular restoration practices.
- **Automated Recycling and Material Recovery Technologies**: Smart recycling systems enable efficient waste sorting and upcycling, increasing circular material use.

By integrating technology and digital solutions, circular restoration initiatives can be monitored, optimized, and expanded efficiently.

Cross-Sector Collaboration for Large-Scale Implementation

No single entity can scale circular restoration efforts alone. Effective collaboration between governments, businesses, non-profits, and academia is essential for replicating successful models at a broader scale.

Key Collaborative Strategies for Scaling Circular Restoration:

- **PPPs**: Governments and businesses work together to fund and implement circular infrastructure projects such as green buildings, regenerative agriculture, and waste-to-energy facilities.
- **Industry-wide Circular Economy Standards**: Establishing universal guidelines for material reuse, product design, and resource recovery ensures consistency across sectors.
- **Knowledge Sharing Platforms**: Open-source databases and industry networks promote the replication of successful circular economy models across regions.
- **Cross-Border Policy Alignment**: Countries align policies to support global trade in recycled materials, circular investments, and sustainable resource management.

Through collaboration and knowledge exchange, circular restoration efforts can be adopted by multiple stakeholders and scaled globally.

Regulatory Support and Policy Alignment

Policies and regulations play a key role in removing barriers to scaling circular economy initiatives by creating an enabling environment for businesses, investors, and communities to participate in large-scale circular restoration projects.

Policy Approaches for Scaling Circular Restoration:

- **Mandatory Circular Design Standards**: Requiring products and infrastructure to be designed for durability, repairability, and recyclability promotes circularity at scale.
- **Incentives for Circular Business Models**: Tax breaks, subsidies, and investment grants encourage businesses to adopt scalable circular practices.
- **Land-Use and Ecosystem Restoration Mandates**: Governments set legal requirements for reforestation, soil restoration, and water conservation, driving large-scale adoption.

- **Circular Economy Reporting and Compliance**: Standardized reporting frameworks ensure that companies and governments track progress toward circular economy goals.

By aligning policy measures with circular economy principles, governments can create long-term regulatory certainty that supports the scaling of ecosystem restoration initiatives.

Community Engagement and Social Inclusion

Scaling circular restoration solutions requires active participation from local communities, ensuring that projects are socially inclusive, economically viable, and locally adapted. Community-driven circular initiatives increase public awareness, foster grassroots action, and build long-term resilience.

Strategies for Community-Led Circular Scaling:

- **Citizen Science and Environmental Stewardship**: Local communities contribute to biodiversity monitoring, waste recovery, and conservation efforts, making circular restoration more scalable.
- **Circular Job Creation and Green Workforce Development**: Training programs equip people with skills in repair, remanufacturing, and ecosystem restoration, expanding employment opportunities.
- **Consumer Engagement in Circular Lifestyles**: Public awareness campaigns encourage waste reduction, responsible consumption, and participation in circular economy programs.
- **Social Enterprises and Community-Owned Circular Projects**: Local cooperatives manage recycling facilities, sustainable agriculture programs, and community-led reforestation efforts.

By empowering communities, circular restoration solutions become scalable, adaptable, and deeply integrated into local economies.

Corporate and Institutional Investment in Circular Restoration

Corporate and institutional investment plays a critical role in scaling circular restoration efforts by mobilizing financial resources, driving innovation, and influencing market trends. As businesses and financial institutions increasingly recognize the economic and environmental benefits of circular economy models, investment in sustainable infrastructure, resource-efficient technologies, and ecosystem restoration projects has grown significantly. However, barriers such as financial risk, policy uncertainty, and short-term profit expectations continue to limit widespread adoption.

To drive large-scale impact, corporations, banks, pension funds, and investment firms must align their strategies with circular economy principles, ensuring that financial decisions support long-term environmental and social resilience. This shift requires clear investment frameworks, public-private collaboration, and standardized impact measurement metrics to attract capital into circular restoration initiatives.

This section explores how corporate and institutional investors can accelerate circular ecosystem restoration, focusing on sustainable investment frameworks, ESG-driven financing, corporate circularity strategies, and risk mitigation measures.

Sustainable Investment Frameworks for Circular Restoration

Institutional investors, including sovereign wealth funds, pension funds, and development banks, are increasingly integrating sustainability criteria into their portfolios. By prioritizing circular economy investments, these institutions help fund projects that promote waste reduction, renewable resource use, and ecological regeneration.

Key Elements of Sustainable Investment Frameworks:

- **Green and sustainable bonds**: Institutional investors allocate capital to projects focused on circular infrastructure, clean energy, and sustainable land use.
- **ESG screening**: Investment portfolios integrate circular economy principles into corporate due diligence processes.
- **Impact investing models**: Capital is directed toward initiatives that deliver measurable environmental benefits alongside financial returns.
- **Circular venture capital and private equity funds**: Investors support startups and businesses that develop circular solutions, such as biodegradable materials, closed-loop manufacturing, and regenerative agriculture.

By embedding circular economy principles into investment decisions, financial institutions drive long-term sustainability and ecosystem resilience.

ESG-Driven Financing and Circular Economy Integration

ESG criteria have become essential for companies and investors seeking to align their financial strategies with sustainable development goals. As regulatory frameworks tighten and consumer demand for responsible business practices grows, corporations and institutional investors are increasing their focus on ESG-aligned investments.

How ESG Financing Supports Circular Restoration:

- **Sustainability-linked loans and bonds**: Corporations receive preferential interest rates when meeting circular economy performance targets, such as reducing resource waste or implementing regenerative practices.
- **Corporate impact funds**: Large companies establish internal investment funds dedicated to circular innovation, waste recovery, and ecosystem restoration.

- **Carbon pricing and offsets**: Companies invest in reforestation, soil regeneration, and carbon capture projects to meet net-zero commitments.
- **Supplier sustainability programs**: Businesses provide financial incentives to suppliers that implement circular product design, sustainable packaging, and waste reduction strategies.

By integrating circular economy principles into ESG financing, businesses and investors create long-term value while reducing environmental impact.

Corporate Circular Economy Strategies and Investment Priorities

Leading corporations are integrating circular economy models into their business operations, supply chains, and investment strategies. These efforts not only support ecosystem restoration but also create cost savings, new revenue streams, and competitive advantages.

Corporate Investment Strategies for Circular Restoration:

- **R&D funding for circular product innovation**: Companies invest in eco-friendly materials, biodegradable packaging, and resource-efficient manufacturing.
- **Industrial symbiosis and resource-sharing initiatives**: Businesses collaborate across industries to repurpose waste streams, reduce resource extraction, and improve efficiency.
- **Corporate reforestation and biodiversity restoration projects**: Firms allocate funding to large-scale tree planting, wetland rehabilitation, and carbon sequestration programs.
- **Circular procurement policies**: Corporations prioritize sourcing recycled, upcycled, or sustainably certified materials, influencing broader market adoption.

By embedding circularity into business models, companies reduce costs, enhance brand reputation, and contribute to global sustainability goals.

Risk Mitigation and Policy Support for Circular Investment

Despite the long-term benefits of circular economy investments, financial risks and policy uncertainties can deter corporate and institutional investors. Addressing these challenges requires risk mitigation strategies, regulatory support, and collaboration between financial stakeholders and policymakers.

Risk Management Strategies for Circular Economy Investment:

- **Blended finance models**: Governments and development banks co-invest with private sector firms, reducing financial risks in high-impact restoration projects.
- **Insurance mechanisms for ecosystem services**: Investors use parametric insurance models to protect against risks related to climate change, biodiversity loss, and resource depletion.
- **Standardized impact measurement and reporting**: Clear performance metrics help businesses and investors track the economic and environmental benefits of circular investments.
- **Regulatory incentives for corporate sustainability**: Governments offer tax breaks, subsidies, and investment grants to encourage circular investment in key industries.

By creating a supportive investment climate, policymakers and financial institutions enable scalable and resilient circular restoration solutions.

Measuring Success: Metrics for Circular Ecosystem Restoration

Ensuring the effectiveness of circular ecosystem restoration efforts requires clear, standardized metrics that can track progress, impact, and long-term sustainability. Measuring success is essential for governments, businesses, investors, and communities to determine whether circular economy principles are being successfully applied to ecosystem regeneration, waste reduction, and resource efficiency.

A well-defined measurement framework provides insights into the economic, environmental, and social benefits of circular restoration initiatives. It enables data-driven decision-making, policy adjustments, and investment strategies to enhance impact at local, national, and global levels. Without quantifiable indicators, it becomes difficult to assess whether projects are achieving their intended goals or if further improvements are needed.

This section explores key metrics for measuring success in circular ecosystem restoration, focusing on environmental impact indicators, resource efficiency benchmarks, economic performance metrics, and social impact assessments.

Environmental Impact Indicators for Circular Restoration

Restoring ecosystems through circular economy principles requires measuring improvements in biodiversity, soil health, air quality, water conservation, and carbon sequestration. These indicators provide insights into how well restoration efforts are supporting ecological resilience.

Key Environmental Metrics:

- **Biodiversity restoration index**: Tracks changes in species richness, habitat connectivity, and ecosystem health before and after restoration.
- **Carbon sequestration levels**: Measures the amount of CO_2 absorbed by forests, wetlands, and regenerated soils to assess climate benefits.

- **Soil health and regeneration**: Evaluates organic matter content, erosion rates, and microbial activity to determine soil restoration progress.
- **Water quality and availability**: Monitors improvements in freshwater resources, reduction of pollutants, and efficiency of water reuse in circular systems.
- **Reduction in pollution and landfill waste**: Quantifies decreases in industrial emissions, plastic pollution, and hazardous waste disposal.

By monitoring environmental impact indicators, stakeholders can assess the effectiveness of circular restoration efforts in regenerating ecosystems.

Resource Efficiency and Circularity Metrics

Circular economy success depends on optimizing resource use, minimizing waste, and closing material loops. Tracking how effectively resources are being recovered, reused, and regenerated helps measure circularity in ecosystem restoration projects.

Key Resource Efficiency Metrics:

- **Material circularity rate**: Measures the percentage of materials recovered and reintegrated into the economy instead of being discarded.
- **Water and energy efficiency ratios**: Assesses the reduction in water and energy consumption through circular water management and renewable energy use.
- **Waste-to-resource conversion rates**: Tracks how much industrial, agricultural, or urban waste is successfully repurposed into new materials or energy.
- **Soil nutrient recycling efficiency**: Evaluates the reuse of organic waste, compost, and bio-based fertilizers to enhance soil fertility.

- **Extended product lifespan indicators**: Measures the durability, repairability, and recyclability of materials used in circular restoration efforts.

By improving resource efficiency and tracking circularity performance, organizations can ensure that materials and ecosystems are used sustainably over time.

Economic Performance and Investment Impact

Financing circular restoration efforts requires measuring economic returns, cost savings, and investment efficiency. Economic performance metrics help governments, businesses, and investors determine whether circular economy investments are financially viable.

Key Economic Metrics:

- **Return on investment (ROI) for circular projects**: Assesses the financial viability of circular infrastructure, regenerative agriculture, and green business models.
- **Cost savings from waste reduction**: Calculates how much money is saved by reducing raw material consumption and increasing resource efficiency.
- **Job creation in circular industries**: Measures the number of green jobs generated by restoration projects, waste management innovations, and sustainable supply chains.
- **Revenue generated from secondary materials**: Tracks the economic value of recycled and repurposed materials within circular systems.
- **Government spending on circular incentives**: Evaluates public funding efficiency for promoting sustainable development and restoration efforts.

By demonstrating economic benefits, circular restoration projects become more attractive to investors, policymakers, and businesses.

Social and Community Impact Assessment

The long-term success of circular restoration efforts depends on community engagement, public awareness, and social inclusivity. Measuring how circular initiatives benefit local populations ensures that projects remain equitable and impactful.

Key Social Impact Metrics:

- **Community participation in restoration efforts**: Tracks the number of volunteers, local businesses, and organizations involved in circular projects.
- **Public awareness and education levels**: Assesses how well communities understand and adopt circular economy principles.
- **Social equity in access to circular jobs**: Measures whether employment opportunities in circular restoration sectors are reaching diverse social groups.
- **Health benefits from ecosystem restoration**: Evaluates improvements in air quality, water cleanliness, and reduced exposure to pollutants in communities.
- **Stakeholder satisfaction and policy alignment**: Surveys business leaders, policymakers, and residents on their perceptions of circular economy initiatives.

Ensuring social benefits and public engagement enhances the long-term sustainability and effectiveness of circular restoration programs.

Conclusion

The integration of circular economy principles into ecosystem restoration offers a transformative approach to sustainable resource management, environmental regeneration, and long-term resilience. Unlike traditional linear economic models, which prioritize extraction, use, and disposal, circular restoration strategies emphasize waste reduction, resource efficiency, and regenerative practices that support both natural ecosystems and economic sustainability.

Throughout this book, we have explored how circular principles can be applied across waste management, water conservation, agriculture, biodiversity protection, infrastructure development, and governance frameworks. Each of these areas demonstrates that closing material loops, adopting nature-based solutions, and implementing circular strategies can help restore degraded ecosystems, improve environmental health, and enhance climate resilience.

Key financing mechanisms, including green bonds, sustainability-linked loans, and impact investing, play a crucial role in scaling circular restoration efforts, ensuring that businesses and governments have the financial resources needed to implement large-scale sustainability initiatives. Moreover, corporate engagement, institutional investment, and public-private partnerships are essential in driving the adoption of circular economy models on a broader scale.

Measuring success through environmental, economic, and social impact metrics ensures that restoration efforts remain effective, accountable, and adaptable to changing conditions. With clear monitoring frameworks and data-driven decision-making, circular restoration projects can achieve greater efficiency, long-term sustainability, and replicability across different regions and industries.

By embracing a circular economy approach to ecosystem restoration, we can simultaneously protect natural resources, enhance economic opportunities, and build resilient communities that thrive in harmony with the environment.

The Future of the Circular Economy in Ecosystem Restoration

Looking ahead, the future of circular economy-driven ecosystem restoration will depend on scaling successful initiatives, advancing innovative technologies, and fostering cross-sector collaboration. As climate change, resource depletion, and biodiversity loss intensify, circular solutions will become increasingly essential for restoring degraded ecosystems, protecting water resources, and ensuring food security.

Emerging technologies such as AI-driven waste management, blockchain for transparent supply chains, and smart water monitoring systems will further enhance the efficiency and scalability of circular restoration efforts. Digital tools will enable real-time tracking of resource flows, improved waste recovery processes, and optimized regenerative land management.

Governments and international organizations will need to establish stronger regulatory frameworks, economic incentives, and policy alignment to accelerate the adoption of circular economy models in ecosystem restoration. Businesses will play a key role by redesigning products, optimizing material use, and investing in circular infrastructure to drive systemic change.

Public engagement and education will also be critical in shifting mindsets toward sustainable consumption, responsible waste management, and community-led restoration projects. By integrating circularity into daily life, societies can reduce environmental impact while improving resilience and economic stability.

Ultimately, the future of circular restoration lies in collective action, innovation, and commitment to long-term sustainability. By leveraging circular economy principles, we can build a world where natural ecosystems, human societies, and economic systems coexist in balance, creating a more regenerative and resilient future for all.

www.ingramcontent.com/pod-product-compliance
Lightning Source LLC
Chambersburg PA
CBHW052135270326
41930CB00012B/2891